HEATH LEDGER

JOHN McSHANE

HEATH LEDGER

HIS BEAUTIFUL LIFE AND MYSTERIOUS DEATH

JOHN BLAKE

Published by John Blake Publishing Ltd,
3 Bramber Court, 2 Bramber Road,
London W14 9PB, England

www.johnblakepublishing.co.uk

First published in paperback in 2008

ISBN: 978-1-84454-633-6

British Library Cataloguing-in-Publication Data:

A catalogue record for this book is available from the British Library.

Design by www.envydesign.co.uk

Printed in Great Britain by CPI Bookmarque, Croydon, CR0 4TD

7 9 10 8 6

Papers used by John Blake Publishing are natural, recyclable products
made from wood grown in sustainable forests. The manufacturing processes
conform to the environmental regulations of the country of origin.

Every attempt has been made to contact the relevant copyright-holders,
but some were unobtainable. We would be grateful if the appropriate
people could contact us.

CONTENTS

PROLOGUE

The New York policeman held the apartment block's large front door open with his hand. His right foot rested firmly against the metal plate at bottom of the door as insurance, just in case a surprise gust of winter night air forced it to slam shut. Two burly paramedics appeared from inside the tall building pushing a trolley and moved briskly past him. The man in front wore a woolly hat pulled down to his ears, his colleague's bald head was uncovered and it almost shone in the dazzling arc lights and countless camera flashes that greeted the pair. On the trolley was a black body bag held in place by four thick straps, all pulled tight around the human being inside.

It was 6.28 p.m. on 22 January 2008. The place was 421 Broome Street in SoHo, New York. The street had been cordoned off by police and the crowds outside the building were forced to wait behind the barriers that had hurriedly been erected. Film crews, photographers, reporters, fans and the just plain morbidly curious were penned back behind them as they watched the sad scene unfold.

Broome Street, although in a fashionable area in that most hip of cities, had suddenly gone from being a comparatively anonymous Manhattan street to an address at the centre of the world's attention. The reason was simple; inside the bag was the body of a 28-year-old man – Heath Ledger, film star.

In the few short hours since his death the news had spread around the globe. From his birthplace in Australia to the United States of America, which had become his home, all were stunned by the news. But it wasn't just in those two countries that people were listening to every small piece of information they could about his untimely death. It was the same in every country where films were shown – and that meant the entire world. He was so young. He had so much to live for. He had everything ahead of him. And yet Heath Ledger was dead.

Most knew him as a tall, handsome young actor with a striking screen presence. Many actors dreamed of possessing such a gift, but it was only ever given to a handful who had been sprinkled with true stardust. A much smaller group knew him as a man who had set out on his chosen career at a precociously early age and succeeded in the most competitive of professions thanks not only to his ability but also to his determination. And an even smaller group knew him as a loving father of a small daughter, whom he adored.

Heath Ledger was already a star when he decided to accept the role in a film dubbed, no matter how often or vigorously the clichéd classification was denied, the 'gay cowboy' movie. *Brokeback Mountain* turned him into a superstar and his life was changed dramatically by it.

All that lay in the past, however, as the paramedics hurriedly moved from the elegant block where Heath Ledger lived and died, across the sidewalk and into the road between parked police cars to the waiting medical examiner's white van with its rear doors already open. They quickly unloaded the body bag and the stretcher it was on into the back of the van and then clumsily struggled to collapse the trolley. After thirty seconds they managed to complete the manoeuvre and the van doors were closed. Heath Ledger was driven away.

CHAPTER 1

SEA, SURF AND GENE KELLY

'One of the most isolated cities in the world.' That was how Heath Ledger would often describe his birthplace of Perth in Western Australia. Its nearest neighbour with a population of over one million, Adelaide, is a staggering 1,307 miles away, and it's closer to Jakarta in Indonesia than it is to big metropolitan centres such as Sydney and Melbourne.

On 11 June 1829 Captain James Stirling, on board a chartered former troop-carrier called *The Parmelia*, founded a colony a short distance inland from the Indian Ocean on the Swan River, named after the native black swans gently gliding across its surface. Stirling had his wife and two young sons aboard – one whom had been born at sea during the long voyage from England – and he pronounced the area that was to become Heath's birthplace, 'as beautiful as anything of this kind I had ever witnessed.'

Stirling had already selected the name 'Perth' for the capital well before the town was officially established, naming it after the Scottish hometown of the then Secretary of State for the Colonies, Sir George Murray.

Although the British formed the majority of the early population and did so for more than a century, after World War II migrants from Italy and Greece, then later the Eastern European countries changed Perth's social mix. Added to them was to be a large number of New Zealanders – given easy access due to their country's relationship with Australia – and Malaysians. It became popular with South Africans too and the phrase 'packing for Perth' was synonymous with wishing to emigrate from the troubled African state. The influx meant that the city's population literally doubled to one and a half million in Heath's short lifetime, making it the fastest-growing city on the continent.

Despite this melting pot, the vast distances involved and the geographical isolation on the Western 'end' of Australia are worth remembering in the life story of Heath Ledger, especially in his early years. He must have felt the contradiction between living in a vibrant major 20th-century city, with all its amenities and comforts, while simultaneously being almost an outpost, in geographical terms at least, from the hub of mainstream cultural and artistic life.

Towns and cities such as Perth, the capital of Western Australia, give young Australians from all over the vast country an almost inbuilt desire to roam across continents with the relaxed matter-of-factness many others might reserve for a trip to the shops. They seem born with a passport in one pocket and a backpack over their shoulders: distance no object. Heath Ledger was to be no different; the world was there for him to explore and enjoy – and that was exactly what he was to do.

All of that lay years in the future, however, when on 4 April 1979 he was born in the St John of God hospital in Subiaco, an inner suburb in western Perth. The hospital dates back to 1897 but by the time Heath arrived it was modern and comfortable, an ideal place in which to enter the world. The city and surrounding area prospered in large part due to its proximity to vast natural resources of gold, diamonds, coal and natural gas, which meant many of the world's leading engineering and mineral development companies had offices there.

While it would be romantic to say that the infant boy was born into hardship and strife and would have to battle against poverty as he grew up before achieving fame, this was not the case. The Ledger name was a well-known one in Perth and Western Australia and the family owned and ran a large foundry which provided many of the metals, raw materials and parts needed to construct the 330-mile-long Perth-to-Kalgoorlie pipeline – one of the longest in the world – supplying water to the arid inland desert, where the Australian gold rush was underway in the late 19th century. In 1903 it started to pump water to prospectors and farmers, and the family name was subsequently synonymous with business success in the following years. Heath's great-grandfather, Sir Frank Ledger, even gave his name to a charitable foundation that was to generously give scholarships to talented students as well as fund universities and pay the fees and travel costs for visiting lecturers.

His parents were racing car driver and mining engineer Kim Ledger and French teacher Sally Ledger Bell (formerly Bradshaw), who was descended from the Scottish Campbell clan, famous – *infamous* in many people's eyes – for their part in the 1692 massacre of the MacDonald family at Glencoe, having accepted their hospitality for days.

For the proud parents there was no problem when it came to choosing a name for their boy, albeit a highly unusual one. Four years earlier they had named their first child Catherine – she came to be known as Kate – after the heroine of the classic Emily Brontë novel, *Wuthering Heights*. This 1847 work, first published under a male pseudonym, as was often the case at the time, chronicles the doomed love of Catherine (Cathy) Earnshaw for the brooding Heathcliff, a dark figure and one of the first anti-heroes in literature, on the bleak Yorkshire Moors. In spite of its initially cool reception – her sister Charlotte's *Jane Eyre* was more enthusiastically greeted – Emily's masterpiece was to make Cathy and Heathcliff one of the most famous sets of lovers ever to spring to life from the pages of a book. So it was that the Ledgers chose their boy's name, shortened in the modern world to Heath, and he was given the middle name Andrew.

According to astrologers, people born under the influence of his star sign of Aries, the Ram, are: 'Noted for courage and leadership qualities, primarily because they are nearly always ready for action. The need for excitement pushes them into new territory – and as long as they are ahead of others while demonstrating confidence, chances are that they will follow. As self-ordained leader of the pack, Aries fight for what they believe to be important. But it's not that Aries are fearless. Their courage is more of a commitment to face their fears and overcome them.' This is a remarkably accurate description of Heath. Hopeful as his parents would have been for their tot's success, even they cannot have foreseen what lay ahead for Heath – who in later years gained two half-sisters, Olivia and Ashleigh, after his parents divorced. A sign of the affection and closeness he always felt for his mother and sisters eventually came when he combined their initials to spell 'KAOS' and had it tattooed on his wrist.

School in the early days was briefly Mary's Mount Primary School in Gooseberry Hill, and then he moved on to Guildford Grammar School in Perth, one of the most prestigious learning academies in Western Australia, if not the whole of Australia. In 1896 a Mr. Charles Harper, an influential figure in Western Australian history, decided to set up a school for his own children and those of surrounding families in his stately home, Woodbridge House. As was often the case in those days of Empire, when the sun never set on the red parts of the globe belonging to Britain, there was only one type of school imaginable for the sons of wealth and influence: an English public school. Harper, like many men around him in those

Colonial days, modelled his school along those lines while seeking to integrate some elements of the new Colonial world, an ethos still in force when Heath was a pupil.

Early classes were taken in the elegant, masculine billiard room of Woodbridge under the guidance of the school's first headmaster, Frank Bennett. Within a very short time it was obvious that the school had to expand and so in 1904 it moved from the Harper family home to its present 100-hectare site on the rolling banks of the Swan River, about 10 miles from Perth. Despite the advances of the ever-enlarging city, the school still had a countryside feel to it even as it entered the modern era and Heath walked through the doors for the first time. The campus is recognised as one of the most picturesque in the country and one of its best-known features, framed by magnificent old London plane trees, is the imposing Chapel of St Mary & St George. Consecrated in 1914, it is recognised as one of the finest examples of Gothic architecture in Australia and young Heath would have been among the generations of 'Guildfordians' in their black blazers with white piping who worshipped there.

For recreation there was a host of sports, including rowing on the nearby river and swimming in an Olympic-sized pool. A brief look at the list of clothing pupils at the £6,000-a-year school must possess amply illustrates its public school heritage in stark contrast to the informal attire of many 'dressing-down' schools. For general wear all boys still need: a school blazer, four blue shirts, four white shirts, two grey mélange trousers, two navy shorts, one house top, one school tie, one house tie, four short grey socks, four long grey socks, one school bag and one school cap. The only item optional on the list – its absence almost a testimony to the Mediterranean climate that Perth enjoys – is a school sweater. A similar lengthy list is required for sports clothing, including one top purely for warm-up activities.

Those sports clothes would have come in handy for the young Heath. Like all schools of its type there was a Cadet Corps, but its military leanings didn't attract him. He was later to admit, 'I didn't want to fight. I thought it was strange that they were teaching kids to shoot automatic weapons.' Instead he veered towards sport, playing both cricket and the hectic, combative Australian Rules football. He excelled, however, at hockey and was good enough to make the school First XI at an early age and as if all that wasn't enough, he was also a fine chess player and became State junior champion at the age of 10. 'He was always five moves ahead of anyone else,' said his proud father – who he would regularly beat, even from an early age.

Despite his family connections it was, in many ways, a typical Australian upbringing for a teenage boy. He earned extra money by washing cars and his family even had a pet kangaroo that they cared for after its mother's death. Away from school he could be found surfing and skateboarding and he was also a keen fisherman. Add to that the bonus of being able to enter the pits with his father at motor racing or motor-biking events and life seemed good for young Heath. He was so adept at sports that he managed to win several titles at local go-karting races.

But it wasn't all sport and the acting bug hit him while still in short trousers. An early taste of the theatre came when he saw his sister Kate, who was later to become a stage director, onstage with Perth's Shakespearian troupe at the city's Globe Theatre. It is impossible to quantify the impact this would have had on his young mind, but at the tender age of 10 he was already in a starring role at the same theatre as Peter Pan, in J M Barrie's classic: the magical story of a little boy who just won't grow up. Other roles followed in *Bugsy Malone*, *Royal Hunt for the Sun* and Laertes in *Hamlet*.

Heath's bedroom in the family home was already covered with modern art posters and when he was given the choice of drama or hockey at school he unhesitatingly chose the former. Some teachers tried to dissuade him, but then, as in later years, he knew his own mind and dismissed their pleading. He later revealed on the school website: 'A few teachers at school tried every opportunity to discourage my participation in drama, basically telling me that I was wasting my time. That kind of made me angry and determined to prove I could achieve the goals I set for myself.'

Despite his undoubted excellence at the sport he later had to admit, 'I don't like telling people I played field hockey. It's real big in Australia for guys, but in America I say I played and everybody goes "Oh, you girl!"'

Along with the sports he thrived at, he was also a movie fan – although he later tried to play that down – and had a special liking for the legendary 'hoofers' Gene Kelly and Judy Garland. His first crush was on Garland in *The*

Wizard of Oz but Kelly in particular, with his ballet poise yet totally masculine grace and power, appealed – especially in the swash-bucking *The Pirate*.

'The first Gene Kelly movie I saw was *The Pirate* and it just blew me away. It's not just Gene Kelly – I'm in love with the energy those movies bring into entertainment. Kelly wasn't the greatest actor and he wasn't a great singer,' he was to say, 'but boy, could he dance! And he had such a strong spirit. He could bring light to the screen and just fill it up. I remind myself of his spirit sometimes when I need to push through on a particular scene.'

As well as Kelly he admired the films of Jack Nicholson, adored Daniel Day-Lewis's performance in the movie *In The Name of the Father* and, for lighter relief, he watched – and always retained a soft spot for – Chuck Norris's martial arts films, especially *Delta Force*.

The theatrical bug had bitten really deep by this time. Perhaps it was the result of another important event in his life, his parents' separation when he was 10. This obviously had a profound effect on Heath, who spent the following years moving between the two of them. He was to call his parents his 'closest friends' and say the split 'wasn't the death of something, but the birth of something else. What I've always looked for is redirection of energy and emotion, and maybe the thrust of that started there.'

If that teenage decision to opt for drama instead of hockey was not proof enough of a new direction in his young life, his father Kim later recalled: 'He was very good at cricket, but hockey was his passion. I thought he would go on with it, but he said, "It won't pay the bills."' After the decision to choose drama at school Kim was to say, 'Heath is extremely dedicated and follows his passions. I picked him up late one night after a rehearsal. He was about 13, and we were lying on his bed, looking at the stars stuck on his ceiling, and he said, "I'm going to have to get used to these late nights; I'm going to do really well in this industry – I love it!"'

It was at 13 that he appeared in a children's television show filmed in Perth, *Clowning Around*, with Aboriginal actor Eddie Dingo – later to be in a *Crocodile Dundee* film – as a boy who runs away to join a circus. This was followed by *Ship to Shore*, again filmed in Perth, and although he was not a regular in the series (about a group of youngsters on a sun-soaked island), Heath went global for the first time as the show was broadcast not only in Australia but the UK, Canada, Germany, Portugal and Latin America.

His burgeoning talent was there for all to see and one person who really sat up and took notice was casting agent Annie Murtagh-Monks, who spotted him in a school production of *Hamlet*. 'He was a very talented young kid and a good one to work with,' was her immediate impression.

In a rather laid-back remark some years later, Heath gave his own take on how he entered the professional acting world: 'I did some little plays in primary school and high school, but even then I never thought about becoming an actor.' Sister Kate, however, was pursuing the craft, and one day when he was 14 he accompanied her to an agent's office. 'The agent was, like, "Nice to meet you, kid; you should audition for this show." I auditioned, and I got it. Suddenly I was a professional actor.'

The TV programme was called *Sweat*, and it was Ledger's first 'professional' audition: 'I was getting paid money and suddenly realised this was something I could do: work hard for five months then take six months off. The leisure time in between was very attractive to me at that age.'

Sweat, which aired in 1996, was a television series filmed in Perth, based on an Australian school for the athletically gifted. It is best remembered now as being Heath's first regular role, as Snowy Boles, a cyclist who happened to be – and here are shades of things to come – gay, the first time a homosexual teenager had been portrayed on Australian television. The show was short-lived, just 26 episodes, and Heath had his first experience of a review that actors just don't cut out and paste in their scrapbooks, not with any pleasure anyway. The influential *Sydney Morning Telegraph* pulled no punches:

> More splutter than sweat so far, with the new drama travelling like a car with a cold engine. The ingredients are in place, with a talented young cast and vibrant art design providing the 'Australian look' so essential to the European sales that will determine the program's fate. What is missing is a bit of heat, which should come with time. In this episode, Snowy

(Heath Ledger) confronts the problem of coming out. The other lads are a bit bemused, not least Snowy's room- and team-mate, Danny (Matt Castelli), who feels the obligatory sense of threat. Sandy (Melissa Thomas) is heartbroken.

In retrospect, it was probably too early in the series to introduce the issue. The actors haven't had enough time to dig their characters into viewers' hearts or, one suspects, their own. The resultant confrontation is oddly sterile, imposed on the characters rather than emerging from inside them. We need to know Snowy better before empathising with his stress. The writing draws on the conventions of coming-out scenes, instead of the particularity of this place and time, so we end up seeing what we have all seen before. It's called cliché. Dramas take notoriously long to warm up. In a timeslot that can only be described as bizarre (what are teens doing at 6.30p.m. on Saturdays?), *Sweat* may take even longer. Time to let out a bit of choke.

There isn't a famous actor or actress in the world who hasn't been the target of a vitriolic pen at some stage in their career, so Heath was no different. In fact, he put it even more harshly than the reviewer: 'I was crap. I remember just burying my face in my hands, thinking, "This is the end, it hasn't even begun."' But he certainly didn't allow himself to become downhearted by the fate of Sweat, or if he was, he didn't let it show.

There were, however, many good times too. Heath taught himself to dance, as he taught himself many other skills, and he was to choreograph a dance routine for a boys' team from the school at a national competition, the Rock Eisteddfod, where the dance teams normally came from all-girl schools. Many of the boys were from farming stock, the school had always been a favourite establishment for farmers spread out over Western Australia to send their sons to, and yet Heath cajoled and charmed his fellow pupils – he stressed it would give them a chance to meet their girl rivals – to such an extent that they won first prize. It was an achievement he always treasured.

'It's a nationwide high-school competition; it's a dance thing. You get about 60 or 80 students. You have to create an eight-minute dance piece to a topic you've picked; you have to create your own sets and costumes. And you've got a month or two to do it. Usually a lot of girls' schools do it. We were the first all-guys' school ever to do it. Our topic was fashion. It was pretty cheesy but we won the competition. I choreographed the whole thing: 60 male students, all farmers at a military school, who had never danced before. We were doing it just to get out of school and go to the competition so we could meet all those girls. We went through all the different aspects of fashion. It was cool, man. These kids had never danced and didn't think they could do it. I remember the first meeting we had. All of them were kind of surly, going, "F**k this, I'm not gonna dance!" I had to literally get up in front of all these surly guys and put on a song and just dance. By the end, when they won the competition, they were so f***ing blown away by it – for starters that they could simply win something but also that they could dance. I guess it was like a Gene Kelly movie, like *Summer Stock*.'

Halfway through eleventh grade, he sat for his graduation exams earlier than his contemporaries and 'got my marks and f***ed off', later admitting, 'I was a bit of a punk at that age; I had a problem with authority.'

Beautiful Perth, with its climate to die for, white beaches nearby and a standard of living to match anywhere in the world, had been outgrown by the strapping young Heath. He was to describe his home city as 'clear blue skies and crystal oceans for miles – paradise,' but since his parents' divorce he had alternated living between them; indeed it was at his stepfather's farm that he first learnt to ride, which was to play an important part in his later career. Now it was time to pack up and move on. His father Kim remembers, 'It broke my heart, we spent our life together playing sports; I'd run him round to this and that. As a parent you participate in everything they do so when they take off, it's like a divorce.'

Divorce or not, as far as Heath was concerned there was a great big world out there waiting to be conquered. He was just 16.

CHAPTER 2

THE LONG ROAD BEGINS

Most teenagers need money for petrol from their parents when they are setting out for a drive and Heath was no exception. But this no ordinary drive: he and his best friend Tom DiCarlo, who he had known since he was 3, and who in later years was to work as his assistant on his films, were leaving Perth and heading east to Sydney – a staggering journey of 2,500 miles across some of the world's toughest and bleakest terrain. No wonder he needed a sub to fill up the tank for the journey down seemingly endless highways, which normally took five days or more – Heath and his pal did it in three. It was, incidentally, the last time the intensely independent Heath was to borrow money from his folks.

The route would have taken him and Tom in their battered Mazda down some of the most famous highways in the country, including the Eyre Highway, with parts so remote that sections of it, marked in white 'piano key' patterns with turning circles nearby, serve as emergency landing strips for the Flying Doctor Service. There is even one stretch of 90 miles without a single bend or turn.

Settlements are, on average, between 120 and 180 miles apart and the two young men would have passed the Nullarbor Plain on the epic journey. The Nullarbor's name says it all: it is derived from the Latin 'nullus' for nothing and 'arbour' for trees. Even the Aborigine name 'Oondiri' means 'waterless.' Tough country, indeed. 'Crossing the Nullarbor' brings to life the outback history of Australia and a popular item on sale at the roadhouses en route are the stickers that proudly proclaim, 'I have crossed the Nullarbor'.

It was a journey most teenagers – even the almost compulsive exploratory Australians – would have viewed with trepidation and self-doubt. Years later, when Heath was a star, he told *Vanity Fair*: 'It wasn't that painful to leave and head for Sydney, not at that age. No matter how good your family life is, you just want out. Perth is the most isolated city in the world, but it's beautiful. I just had to move on. It's always been like that for me. I've always kept going, going, going. I'm sure my parents were really concerned, but they were wise enough not to show it to me too much. They knew they were not going to stop me. They knew I was going to go. They're amazing. They really just f***ing let me fly! My dad loves being a father. He has to be a father, which I love and hate. I guess it started when I left home, but our relationship went from being in each other's face to being best friends. I guess that comes from understanding him as an adult now that I'm an adult. It's amazing when you come to accept each other's mistakes and let each other make them.'

He had to admit that, 'Looking back I'm amazed that my parents were lenient and understanding, but I was a kid who was going to do it anyway. It was either going to be the hard way or the easy way, and I think they knew that.' His realistic assessment was: 'I knew early on that no one is going to come knocking on your door, that you have to make your own luck – you have to go out there and knock yourself; it doesn't come easy. But I am respectful of the fact that my parents let me follow my dreams. All I had was 69 cents in the bank, plus a bit of cash my parents gave me.'

What he did have, at least, was a place to rest his weary head when he reached Sydney. On the set of *Sweat* he had met and become friendly with New Zealand-born actor Martin Henderson. Although he was four and a half years older than Heath, the two hit it off and became friends. When Henderson – who was later to find fame as the male lead in the chilling *The Ring* with Naomi Watts – returned to Sydney, he contacted Heath and urged him to travel to the city and try his luck on a wider stage. Importantly he was able to provide the offer, which was readily accepted, of a roof over their heads.

Heath arrived at the Bondi apartment carrying just one small bag of luggage and – in almost a caricature of a teenage Australian – a surfboard. It was soon to come in handy. He was not one for the typical teenage trick of lying in bed until noon. Instead, a combination of his vast energy and perhaps a little bit of that private-school education ethos would see him rise sometimes at 6a.m. and head straight down to the beach to catch the sunrise waves.

This is how he summed it up: 'You don't need that much to survive in Australia. My lifestyle was: wake up, eat a bit and walk down to the beach and go for a surf, then just go out for jobs – I loved the whole process of it.' But there was work to be done too, and it was a surfing setting that provided Heath's debut in a movie, in the 1997 film *Blackrock*, directed by Steve Vidler and written by Jack Enright. This was, however, far from a sunny boy-meets-girl frolic on golden sands, a film made more with the intent of showing off the tanned bodies of young surfers and their girlfriends rather than purveying any message. The reason that it subsequently caused controversy in Australia was because it was based on the real-life rape and then murder of a young girl by a gang of macho-male surfers and many people, especially those in the girl's hometown, felt the making of the film without her family's consent was in bad taste, to say the least.

Heath played Toby, one of the rapists, and *Blackrock* was released nationwide just days after his eighteenth birthday and, importantly, it premièred at the prestigious Sundance Film Festival, founded by actor Robert Redford in America. For all the controversy it caused at the time over its examination of the ethos of the beach-life and values enjoyed by many young Australians, it subsequently, and perhaps understandably, is best remembered for being Heath's début on the big screen.

In the same year he also appeared a long way down the casting-list in a Disney-style comedy about a friendly dog – called with a great lack of originality, *Paws* – who holds the key to a lost fortune. The dog's voice was provided by Scottish comedian Billy Connelly. Heath's role, as a student playing Shakespeare's Oberon in a play-within-a-play, was so small that he only appears on the credits in the 'in alphabetical order' section. Then, of course there had been the almost mandatory appearance – albeit fleetingly – in an Aussie soap.

The sunshine of the country and the attractive young actors it boasts have combined to make Australia one of the leading makers of soap operas in the English-speaking world. A job was a job, however, and young Heath appeared in about 10 episodes of *Home and Away* as Scott Irwin, a 'bad boy' type. Yet again he was to play a surfer. 'I had to eat: I was starving! So I played some rebel teenager who came into town and slept with Sally. Actually, I think I was the first to sleep with Sally,' was his summary of the role.

He was far from satisfied with those early appearances, so much so that he even asked his mother for reassurance. 'It was terrible – I was terrible in it. Back then, I couldn't act to save myself. I even remember asking my mom, "I'm not very good in it, I'm really bad." I was waiting for her to say, "No, hon, you're not, you're just fine."' But he didn't get the answer he was expecting: 'She was like, "Well, you know, it doesn't matter."'

At least he realised there was room for improvement: 'That's a step forward; I can understand what's good and bad. I can begin to study what I'm doing wrong. I'm blinking too much, I'm not really listening to them; I'm just saying the lines. I started to change it myself.' But there was no way that he was going to remain in the soap – his big break was just around the corner. On 9 June 1997 an Australian media gossip column carried a brief item halfway down its list of tittle-tattle:

> Network Ten has signed a major new drama series, called *Roar*, which is in production at Warner Bros on the Gold Coast for Universal and Fox in the United States. Created and produced by Shaun Cassidy, brother of the former teen idol David Cassidy, and Ron Koslow (*Beauty and the Beast*), it's a *Braveheart*-style blockbuster about warring clans in Ireland in 400 AD. With a US-Aussie cast, including Heath Ledger (*Blackrock*), Lisa Zane (*ER*, *LA Law*), *The Burning Zone*'s John St Ryan and a guest appearance by Melissa George, *Roar* will air on Ten early next year.

Although filmed in Australia the series had a Celtic setting with Heath as a prince, often clad in a loincloth, who battles magical enemies and beautiful maidens in AD 400, while attempting to bring warring tribes together as they battle to drive the Roman forces out of the country. It was a mélange of styles seen in films ranging from *Braveheart* to *Highlander* to *Star Wars* – and it was to go international. Shaun Cassidy knew all about being a teenage heart-throb. Like his half-brother David, he'd had a spell as a teen idol and he was well aware that his series needed a drop-dead gorgeous star to carry it, the kind of guy that men and, very importantly, young girls would be keen to watch in this pivotal role. And Heath was exactly the type of young lead he had in mind.

Also in *Roar* was Melissa George, then a much bigger name than Heath due to her years in *Home and Away*, and she gave an interview to one Sunday newspaper on her thoughts at landing her role as Molly, a young Celtic orphan. At the end of the article one of the first quoted remarks from Heath about his acting appears. It is brief and very much to the point: 'The way I look at it, it's just another job. But you can't help notice it's different ... it's big, we've got huge sets and we've got a huge budget.' It was also a part that he almost failed to get.

Heath later revealed that he had been to one audition in Australia and, 'I thought I did a fairly good job. They rang my agent a couple of days later and said they were really interested in me for the role of Conor and they wanted to fly me to LA for the final audition. I was working on a TV series in Sydney, so the only possible time they could get me to California was on a weekend. I got there on a Friday night and didn't sleep, because my internal clock was off. I did the audition the next morning, and it was pretty intense for me because we don't do it the same way in Australia.

'The room was packed with suits,' he said of that Californian screen-test. 'After every shot, they swarmed together like a pack of ants on a sweet biscuit, whispering. It was definitely not my best performance, but something must have gone right. All the producers and representatives from Fox and Universal Television were there, and I was really sweating it out. I got through it, but even Shaun [Cassidy] told me it wasn't a very good audition. I jumped right back on the plane, getting back into Sydney when it was Monday morning there, it was like going through time-travel.'

Two weeks later he learnt that he had landed the part: 'I was blown away. It wasn't until a week later that it really sank in. I loved *Braveheart*, and if I hadn't gotten this part, I would have felt it was a real shame. It really fits me, and I love doing it. It's a physically demanding job. Recently, we spent a whole day just doing scenes of running, fighting and riding horses through a forest. The characters are always fighting out of passion or for a cause, whether it's in retaliation for lost family members or to unite tribes. A few episodes don't have much action at all, and that's what's good about this. It's a very emotional show as well. I'm half-Scottish and I have some Irish blood in me, so I've had a fair amount of history pumped through me by my grandparents. Still, I took out a lot of books on Druidism and things like that, just to have a solid background. That way, when you're on the set, you know what you're supposed to be doing and thinking.'

It was clear that he had the acumen to realise that the series, with its massive Celtic connotations, would appeal in his homeland when he told an American questioner, 'They've got a big feel for things like *Braveheart* and *Riverdance*, and I think the whole world has been swept away by that era. It's the fashionable thing right now, but I think everyone has developed a taste for it.'

'Heath was probably the youngest actor we saw,' Shaun Cassidy admitted. 'We'd envisioned Conor as a 22- or 23-year-old guy, but Heath changed our minds. You have to believe that he's a boy who's still got a lot to learn. But when the chips are down, he's going to stand up in front of people who are a lot older and say, "I'm in charge and you are going to follow me." And he's got that quality.'

Another who came to admire his work was the series' stunt co-ordinator Danny Baldwin, who taught him the horse-riding and fighting skills: 'He was a quick learner and by the end of filming he could ride bareback with a sword. He was probably the most talented actor I've worked with,' he said.

Fortunately, Heath adapted quickly to the filming, involving as it did a lot of work on foot and horseback in the rough Australian terrain: 'I had to wear leather pants and this little leather top with chains and stuff. We were shooting in extreme heat and riding horses. The one good thing about it was usually when you're on a set in costume you have to watch where you're sitting and take care not to get it rumpled and not get food on your clothes. But I was in a Celtic roughneck outfit and I could lie around on the ground or get dirty and they wouldn't care.'

The new series launched him into that unknown and ruthless territory known as American prime-time television. It's where fortunes are made and careers can soar to stratospheric heights – or plummet mercilessly. This mid-evening slot is where the biggest audiences lay and that means the largest targets for the advertisers. Ratings are the Gods in this portion of TV Heaven, but also playing their part is the powerful range of television critics across the country.

There were some who found *Roar* predicable and were less than enthusiastic in their praise for the hour-long first episode, while others warmed to its mix and welcomed it to the screens. What the critics were united in, however, was their approval of Heath's performance and none of them decided to stick the knife, or perhaps it should be the broadsword, into him. The *New York Times* guardedly said: '*Roar* obviously hopes to steal some of the fire of the cult hits *Hercules* and *Xena* with their mythical sword-wielding heroics... *Roar* has only two chances for success: Mr. Ledger, who is being carefully positioned as a heart-throb (the little blond braid hanging over his right ear serves as a ready-made trademark) will have to come through in that role. Or this series will have to embrace its inner kitsch.'

The *Baltimore Sun*'s verdict was: 'Comparisons to *Hercules: The Legendary Journeys* and *Xena: Warrior Princess* are inevitable, but while it has its tongue-in-cheek moments, *Roar* seems to take itself a bit more seriously than either: It's hard to imagine Conor helping start the

Olympics or entering the Mr. Known World pageant. Conor is all youthful naiveté and uncertain bravado; he's not sure he can – or wants – to be a leader, but he's willing to try. Australian newcomer Ledger fits the part well; he comes across as brave and a bit foolish, but not cocky.'

And the *Chicago Sun-Times* added: 'Rumbling through the summer rerun season like a sudden thunderstorm, *Roar* refreshes the parched prime-time landscape with gusts of drama and torrents of heart-pounding action... Conor, played with modesty and fury by Australian actor Heath Ledger, loses his family when a rival clan led by King Gar attacks during a wedding feast and massacres King Derek, his queen, his first-born son and the bride... *Roar* delivers rousing battle scenes, outstanding art direction, fair-to-good performances and a medium-depth premise that should generate plenty of high-energy stories.'

Once the reviews were in, Heath pondered on the nature of his growing fame while referring to himself in the third person, as if writing a review: 'Heath Ledger hasn't changed, but Heath Ledger has learned a lot,' he said. 'Of course you learn a lot – I've done a couple of television series and films, and it's all building up. To tell you the truth, it doesn't bother me. A lot of people jump up and down and say, "Hollywood! Hollywood!" I wouldn't mind staying in Australia all my life, working on Australian films and working in the Australian industry. It's growing, it's huge. Hollywood would be great because that's where all the dollars are, but life is not about money – as long as you are having fun and the roles are important to you.'

Something else that was 'important' to him was one of the actresses in *Roar*, the dark-haired Lisa Zane, who played devious Roman emissary Queen Diana, with whom he began a relationship off-screen. At 6'3", Heath towered above the 5' tall Lisa. Just as striking was the difference in their ages; she was born almost 18 years to the day before him. It didn't seem to make any difference to Heath, who throughout his life showed no inhibition about dating women older than himself, indeed he revelled in their company although this was an area – like many in his private life – that he was reluctant to openly discuss.

When shooting in Australia finished, and with the same casualness with which he climbed into the battered old Mazda a few years earlier to head for Sydney, Heath followed Zane, the older sister of *Titanic* actor Billy Zane, back to her Los Angeles base. 'I came to America because I followed a girl,' he said, years later. 'I fell in love and followed my heart, and that's purely what got me to LA. I figured as long as I was there, I would continue my career path.'

If he was hoping to set Hollywood alight at the same rate of knots as he had progressed through the Australian acting scene he was to be disappointed, however. Down Under actors were hot, following the success of Guy Pearce and Russell Crowe in *LA Confidential*, but Heath's summary of the situation was a fairly low-key. His verdict was simply – 'I'm in the boiling pot.'

CHAPTER 3

A VERY GOOD YEAR

1999 was to be a good year for Heath Ledger. If some have felt that the period between Roar and his two hits that year formed a lull in his professional life it should be emphasised that any such conclusion would be false as it fails to take into account the breakneck speed of his career.

Some actors spend years 'resting' or, even if they are in work, hoping for recognition by a wider public. Heath Ledger was still a teenager and even in the most frantic of worlds, the movie business, he was careering ahead at an astonishing rate. He may have spent some 10 months 'bunkering down' in Los Angeles after moving from Australia, but as always, he was waiting for the right property to come along. This was a characteristic that, with a few exceptions, was to stay with him throughout his career.

In March he had already been named by the influential *Entertainment Weekly* among their list of young movie stars to watch, or as they called it: 'Who's Who in Hollywood High'. Alongside him were stars such as Kirsten Dunst, Tobey Maguire, Reese Witherspoon and Jake Gyllenhaal. But it was the two films released that year, although shot in the previous one, which brought him to a wider cinematic audience and were, in a way, to sum up the years ahead: one was as Australian as Bondi Beach and the other pure Hollywood, razzamatazz and all. First, the Australian film: *Two Hands* was written by Gregor Jordan, who was also to direct it, his first major film. It was essentially a crime caper with Heath playing the lead role of Jimmy, who is in debt to local gangster Pando, played by the experienced actor Bryan Brown. Set in and around Sydney – beginning in the infamous red-light district of Kings Cross – strip-club worker Jimmy is approached by local mob boss Pando (Brown), who says he has work for him. He gives Jimmy $10,000 to deliver to a woman in Bondi and when she appears not to be home, he foolishly goes for a swim on the beach, where the money is stolen by a gang of street kids, leaving him in big trouble with Pando and his heavies.

Jimmy comes up with a plan to pay off the debt by robbing a bank and he gets the money he needs, escaping in a stolen car. The vehicle has a radio bumper sticker on it, and while he is driving, he hears that he has won the station's prize of, yes, $10,000. Eventually, after several more twists and turns, Jimmy gets the girl and Pando gets his just rewards. The film was so well received that it won several awards in Australia.

Director Jordan, who was later to make *Ned Kelly*, with Heath in the title role, knew all along that the actor was perfect for the central role of hero Jimmy. During the making of the film in 1998 he and Heath described how he flew to Los Angeles, determined to land his first-choice for the role, a somewhat paradoxical situation in that an Australian director was going to America to persuade a fellow countryman to appear in a role back home. Especially as the actor, Heath, had gone to California to further his career! First, Jordan took him to Hamburger Hamlet at 9201 West Sunset Boulevard in West Hollywood and even later went skiing with him to convince Heath that the part was the right one for him. The skiing may not have been all that necessary as Heath later admitted he knew the part was right for him immediately after the burger!

After months of reading up to a dozen scripts a week he wanted something different and better than was being offered. Or, as he put it, he 'just wanted to crack a film.' Ironically as he sat in Los Angeles it was an offer from his homeland that appealed most and over those burgers the men talked films. 'I fired a million questions at him,' recalled Heath 'like, if this film was a colour, which would it be? What tone?'

What clinched it for him, though, was agreeing with the director that the 'feel' of the film should have the same mood and energy captured in the opening sequence of *Saturday Night Fever*, one of the biggest film hits of all time, with shots of John Travolta's shoes pounding the city pavements and others pulling back as he struts his stuff: 'I knew we had something going then. I used a lot of the characteristics of my friends and how I remembered them being at 14, and being oblivious to things and life. I kind of tried to look at everything through a kid's eyes; I tried to play him just as a little boy stuck in this crazy world where everything's new and innocent to him.' Again he spoke of himself in the third person when he added, 'Heath Ledger at that age had experienced a lot in life, so I had to take that all back and throw it away. I had to become new and fresh, and that was a lot of fun. I was really honoured that Gregor gave me the opportunity to play that character because previous to that in Australian TV or theatre I'd just get cast as the blond kid.'

The making of the movie – described by its director as, '*Goodfellas* in shorts and thongs' – was not without its problems. According to Jordan, the shoot had been: 'a f***ing nightmare. The film is set over two days in the middle of a Sydney summer. But the start of filming last April coincided with the wettest autumn in something like 50 years – this was the autumn that broke El Nino.' It was a case of money going down the drain, literally, as the cancellation fees mounted. 'But when I saw a final print on Monday, it really looked like a hot summer.' That impression was helped by doses of artificial sweat and superimposed grasshopper sounds in the background.

It was all to good effect. The film, likened by one critic to, 'An Australian *Lock Stock and Two Smoking Barrels*', swept the board at the Australian Film Institute Awards in

November 1999 with wins in the Best Film, Best Director and Best Original Screenplay categories, and earned Heath a nomination for Best Actor in a Leading Role. Heath arrived at the AFI Awards in a dark-black suit with velvet trimmings and dark sunglasses, looking, as one report at the time put it, 'very Hollywood' with his co-star Rose Byrne and director Jordan. But he left empty-handed with the award going to another newcomer, Russell Dykstra, for his performance as the troubled son in *Soft Fruit*. It also merited a place at The Sundance Film Festival and was the second time that a film featuring the now 'veteran' 20-year-old had been shown there.

In all, it featured at several film festivals throughout the world, where it was well received. Yet the film's very 'Australian-ness' (one of its strengths) proved to be a barrier when it came to achieving international success. Heath was forced to admit, 'Australians have a huge slang which Americans just would not understand. It's not they don't want to get it – it's just that they haven't lived in Australia and they just can't. It just didn't work.

'At Sundance there would be 12 Aussies in the audience and 100 Americans, and the Aussies would be losing it and the Americans would be looking at each other and going, "Was that funny? Did I miss something?" and just kind of chuckling. It's so Australian that Americans wouldn't have an idea what we were talking about.'

Heath could be forgiven – if he needed to be – for that 'very Hollywood' look at the Australian film awards. He had scored big-time with his other release of the year: the

American-made *10 Things I Hate About You*. William Shakespeare's comedy, *The Taming of the Shrew*, about a headstrong woman and the man who tries to tame her, provided the inspiration for many films in the course of cinema history. The lovers paired together on different occasions had included Mary Pickford and Douglas Fairbanks, Elizabeth Taylor and Richard Burton, and John Wayne and Maureen O'Hara. There had even been some musical versions, the most notable being Cole Porter's marvellous *Kiss Me, Kate*. So when *10 Things...* opened in early spring it had an impressive tradition to maintain – and it managed to do so with critics and the public alike. The *Hollywood Reporter* was one of the first on the scene when it said:

A high school comedy-romance based on a William Shakespeare play – what could be hotter? Touchstone Pictures' freewheeling, frequently knuckleheaded reworking of *The Taming of the Shrew* features a bright, beauteous young cast, but it's not one for serious fans of the Bard. *10 Things I Hate About You* is destined to score a solid hit with the target audience during the holiday weekend. It stars Julia Stiles as Katarina Stratford, a combative, brainy, unpopular teen notorious among her classmates for harassing teachers, ploughing over opponents on the soccer field, backing up and smashing into expensive cars and never dating. There's plenty of silliness to the film's irreverent approach, from elaborate physical gags to such showstoppers as erotic school counsellor Ms. Perky (Allison Janney). There's also plenty of hunkiness on display in the reluctant tamer of Kat, long-haired smooth-talking Aussie import Patrick Verona (Heath Ledger).

The *New York Post* opined:

It's a romp that strip-mines a dozen teen romantic comedies, shamelessly recycling whole scenes from genre classics like *Ferris Bueller's Day Off* and *Animal House*. But still, *10 Things* is a funny movie, cute and genuinely romantic.

The *Washington Post* went even further, headlining their story: 'Shakespeare In Seattle; Why to Love *10 Things I Hate*'. They gave 10 reasons to like it, and No. 3 was:

Decent guys. The boy side of the Shakespearean equation is also neatly evoked: Besides the self-loving Joey (really a minor figure), the gist of the plot follows Cameron James (Joseph Gordon-Levitt of *3rd Rock From the Sun* in the movie's version of Lucentio) as he contrives to get brooding hunk Patrick Verona (Aussie Heath Ledger as the movie's gentleman of Verona, Petruchio) to take out Kat because Kat and Bianca's father has decreed that Bianca can't date till Kat does...

The *Village Voice* verdict was:

> Stiles and her underage Petruchio (Australian actor
> Heath Ledger, as hunky as his name) are charismatic
> and bold enough to carry any romantic comedy. And
> that, plus one really funny joke about the Bard
> himself, is plenty.

The film was well received critically in Britain too, even
by the upmarket papers. The *Independent on Sunday* said
it was the 'best High School movie in years' and it was the
Observer's Movie of the Week. It was a hit with the public
too, easily recouping its costs and quickly making a healthy
profit. Only the Keanu Reeves blockbuster *The Matrix*
prevented it from reaching the Number One spot in the
USA film charts when it hit the cinemas.

Heath's co-star Julia Stiles best summed up the mood of
the young women who flocked to the film: 'Heath has a very
strong personality. He radiates something that draws people
to him. He's also very sexy.' One of the scenes that captured
filmgoers' hearts came when he publicly sings of his love at
a sports stadium. In America, the waspish film critic Roger
Ebert was so taken with it that he wrote, 'I like the sweet,
tentative feeling between Ledger and Stiles. He has a scene
that brings the whole movie to an enjoyable halt. Trying to
win her heart he waits until she's on the athletic field and
then sings "I Love You Baby" over the PA system, having
bribed the school's marching band to accompany him. Those
scenes are worth the price of admission.'

Heath's rendition of the song came after he clambered over the open-air seats at the stadium and he explained how he made the scene memorable: 'I'm not usually a singer, but I was a singer that day; I felt like a rock star for a day. We went into a studio and put it down on track and then we did the whole classic thing which they used to do in old musicals, which is we'd take it out and they'd play it back and put it over loudspeakers, and I did this dance number up and down the staircase while I was singing the song.'

Filming of *10 Things…* lasted 8 weeks and the $100,000 he was paid was to bankroll him for a year in Los Angeles. Surprisingly Heath found Stateside shooting less stressful in one way than Australian filming. He told his old school website: 'In Australia budgets and time constraints tend to be tighter. It puts pressure on the cast and crew to perform, regardless of weather conditions, local problems or whatever. This translates into a different work tempo.'

The film enabled him to reflect on his life – and his new cropped hairstyle – 'I just wanted to change my look' – midway through the year. 'I always wanted to be an actor but I never planned to move or go anywhere with it. I just did it as it arose at the time. I'd follow my instincts and follow the path that I was already on and it just kept leading me places. I don't like to stop and think about it, analyse it. I like to be surprised where I am at the end of it and then stop and finally go, this is where I'm at – I like that feeling.'

After living in Los Angeles for two years, he said that it had been fun to suddenly feel a part of Hollywood, to finally, 'contribute something. I remember driving to the première and I just had this grin because I'd been to so many première parties over the years. And even though I was invited, I'd never had a night of my own and that night was mine... There was no other movie coming out except for mine and it felt good!'

Life in Los Angeles wasn't all roses, he admitted, though; in fact he called it, 'a tough nut to crack. It's tough, really tough. It's tough on your soul, tough on everything. I see this around me but I was lucky because I had really good people around me, really good friends, lovely, lovely, lovely people. You can live anywhere in the world with lovely people. I was waiting to find this big, intimidating, this full-on world – and it was... all these people in their rich cars and their attitudes, the pretentiousness. But then, it never gets to me because the second I got here, I just saw straight through it... I never sat in an office with a big producer and got intimidated because he was a producer; because I always look straight through them and see them as 6-year-old kids. It's just a big high school, with rumours and (complaining) and fashions; it's just that.

'And all the people who are here running the show used to be my age not long ago, and they're just playing and pretending to have these roles in the industry. And it's hilarious; it's funny. I just find the humour in it, I guess, which keeps me going.'

There was still the air of the guy who walked into the

apartment carrying a surfboard, when he added, 'I never look a week further ahead, never. I don't care. I just want to keep doing what I do. It'll take me some place and it's always some place interesting.' He expanded his views on his success in a fascinating interview with the *Sunday Telegraph* in Australia:

It's all still sinking in now – what's going on, where I am and who I am. I keep on repeating this: I rarely think further forward than a week. I certainly don't expect anything; I just do my job and it's kind of taken me here. I find all of that a little weird, but I just try and completely separate myself from that side of things. The only time I realise or think about it is when it's presented to me, as in these situations. So I just try and take it as it comes. I hate reading too much about other people. I don't want to feel over-exposed, either.

He also went some way towards explaining that apparent 'inactivity' in Los Angeles in that he wanted, 'to be very selective, though I didn't have a lot to select. But I thought that one's first foray on to the movie scene had to be something very particular to your career ambitions. At the time, the only movies out there were these teen genre movies, and to me, *10 Things* had a great story and character, and a character I knew I could do and represent well. I also knew it would serve as a great contrast to *Two Hands*.'

It helped that he was allowed to play an Australian character for his first Hollywood movie. 'That was the director's idea. From the very first audition, he asked me to test in my natural voice because he liked it. I wasn't there for the two weeks of rehearsals and I didn't know any of the cast,' he explained. He used this experience to help him play the rebellious outsider in the film: 'That's exactly how I played it. I turned up on the set, they were three days into shooting and everyone was checking me over and I was doing the same to them, and that's the same as what my character goes through in the movie, so I used those feelings to play him.'

Heath had studied *The Taming of the Shrew* at school and although the two are very different, he had also seen the Richard Burton and Liz Taylor film. He admitted he had taken some elements of the fiery Welshman's performance on board, but sensibly added, 'Of course, I couldn't play him as a drunk – not in a Disney movie.'

Despite all the glitz surrounding the première of his films in Australia, Heath, who was now handled by CAA, one of the world's top agents, was still able to say happily, 'I have good friends around me who have nothing to do with the industry. Like, right now, I've got all my mates from Perth who've come over. As soon as I finish my press I forget it and I hang out with them. We're like a group again.'

Nevertheless he was aware that Los Angeles was a great base and he explained his motives for moving there to capitalise on the reaction to *Roar*: 'Sometimes, it can take friggin' years for that [success] to happen. So I went straight over there, I got myself a really good agency. It wasn't a decision to go there for the reason of becoming a superstar or getting paid more money or anything like that; it was just where the ball was rolling. It was leading that way and that's what I do in life – I just keep following it where it takes me; I follow my instincts. I jumped on the opportunity. The iron was hot, so I struck.

'A lot of the scripts that you read over there these days are just stupid. Because so many scripts are getting green-lit, they're being written really fast. In a month they'll write a script and you can just tell that; you can pick it up from the stupid storyline, the stupid characters and little things that they could sell the movie on. A script would have, like, two little cool ideas, and that's it. I wasn't up for that; I was after a movie that had a good storyline, good characters that had true emotions; that was honest, and there just wasn't a lot of that out there. Fortunately, the reason why Shakespeare gets redone over and over again and why he's in fashion and cool is because the guy could write!'

Indeed. And he amplified his views when he stated, 'In a way, it's introducing the teen market to a mature subject, to mature literature, in a nice way. Obviously, they couldn't adapt Petruchio to his ruthless self. It wouldn't come across, it wouldn't wash. The way I had to adapt it was instead of Petrucio traditionally being a drunk and arrogant, I made him drunk in flavour, drunk on life.'

Intriguingly he had also noticed a different attitude to those seeking to climb the ladder, an observation made by many British actors and performers too over the years: 'I find that Americans love to help and promote, they love to see people succeed. They help and they push and they love it. But in Australia it's the "tall poppy syndrome." It's really ridiculous. So many actors they build up and then they love to pull the carpet out.'

The speed with which he became a hot item in Hollywood, driven from meeting to meeting, nevertheless brought a smile to his face: 'I jumped on a plane and there were, like, 12 agency meetings in one week. I'm just this little kid from Perth walking in there and, like, they're ringing up on the way to the meetings saying, "What does he like to eat? What does he like to drink?" And I'd go, "Um, cookies and Coke?" Then you'd turn up and there'd be a big tray of cookies and Coke!'

If the plaudits from reviewers and public alike around the world in 1999 were to be matched, something special would be needed in 2000. And who better to provide it than the biggest star Australia has ever produced, old Mad Max himself, Mel Gibson?

CHAPTER 4

A NEW 'FATHER' – MEL GIBSON

It's one of the ironies of the film world that Mel Columcille Gerard Gibson – the biggest film star ever to come from Down Under – was actually born on 3 January 1956, in Peekskill, upstate New York. The sixth of 11 children in a devout Catholic family, Australian blood ran strongly through his veins, though, and his father Hutton moved the family to New South Wales when he was just 12, a migration funded by compensation Hutton received for an injury at work plus his cash win on a US game show.

The young Mel was a hell-raiser, a trait that has reappeared throughout his life, sometimes at the most unexpected times, but he attended drama school and despite eventually finding fame in harum-scarum films won early admiration, not just for his strong good looks but also his acting ability.

Fame came big time with the international release in 1980 of *Mad Max*, a road story of savagery and retribution in post-Apocalyptic Australia. It turned out to be a sensation and earned over $100,000,000 at the box office, approximately 250 times more than it cost to make. Indeed, it wasn't until *The Blair Witch Project* some 20 years later that it was surpassed in the cost-to-profit ratio stakes. It spawned two follow-ups: *Mad Max 2: The Road Warrior* and *Mad Max: Beyond Thunderdome* and this trio alone would have earned Gibson a place in movie history, but there was more to come.

Superstardom arrived in the shape of Gibson's four *Lethal Weapon* films, in which he and Danny Glover played a pair of mismatched Los Angeles cops: Glover, all domesticated and aging, Gibson suicidal and energetic. The films may not have actually been the first 'buddy-cop' movies but they set the benchmark for combining tension, action and humour in an irresistible blockbusting package.

Gibson also appeared in a host of other films such as *Ransom*, *Gallipoli*, *Bird on a Wire* and *The Year of Living Dangerously*, all part of a catalogue that placed him at the peak of his profession. But he moved onto yet another level with 1995's *Braveheart*, which he both starred in and directed. This time it wasn't just the cash registers that illustrated the film's success: it collected five Oscars including Best Picture and Best Director for Gibson.

The film wasn't without its critics, artistic and historical, yet these observations were to be as nothing compared to the storm Gibson was to cause in 2004 with the release of

The Passion of the Christ, the film he directed and co-wrote about the crucifixion which was later criticised for its savagery and its alleged anti-Semitism. All that lay years ahead, however, when in 1999 location shooting began in South Carolina on *The Patriot* – the movie that showed to all and sundry, as if there was any doubt by this time, that Heath Ledger was definitely playing with the 'big boys'.

It wasn't just Gibson's name on the billboards that meant this was a film with some quality meat on its bones: the screenplay was written by Academy Award-nominee Robert Rodat, who wrote *Saving Private Ryan*, and German-born director Roland Emmerich, best known for *Independence Day*, was in charge behind the camera.

Set in the 1770s Gibson played a former hero of the French and Indian Wars, Benjamin Martin, who had renounced fighting forever to raise his large family in peace. He vehemently opposes going to war against the English, although he sympathises with the cause, for the simple reason that as a widower he has seven children to care for and without him there will be no one to look after them.

His eldest son Gabriel, played by Heath, has no such qualms. He is stirred by the cause and, despite his father's opposition, joins the fight against the Redcoats. The outcome, from the filmgoer's point of view, is hardly surprising in that young Gabriel eventually loses his life and Benjamin seeks justice and revenge, both for his dead son and the fledgling nation.

As with *Braveheart* it wasn't long before the historical

contradictions, some would say plain mistakes, of the script were being criticised but most cinema-goers cared little for the carping. As far as they were concerned it was a Mel Gibson action blockbuster with a message permeating the action. It also enabled audiences the world over to ask, 'Hey, who's the good-looking kid with that "something about him" who plays Mel's son?'

Yet it was a role that Heath almost didn't land.

1999 had certainly been a good year, but his two hits – *Two Hands* and *10 Things I Hate About You* – hadn't become thunderous successes by the time he auditioned for *The Patriot* against actors such as Ryan Phillippe, Elijah Wood and Joshua Jackson. Heath was later to admit that he had been hanging around LA for the best part of a year, living off Pot Noodles at the time and rejecting most of the material he was offered: 'I sat on my ass for a year because I didn't want to get caught in that [teen movie] genre and it just wasn't very good material anyway.' He came close to a couple of roles – notably the one which eventually went to Matt Damon in *All the Pretty Horses* – and that of the Devil in *End of Days*, one of Arnold Schwarzenegger's last movies before moving into politics, until a new director came on board and Gabriel Byrne won the role. 'So I got close to things and then the rug was pulled out from under my feet, usually for reasons like I wasn't a name or I was too young.'

He himself was forced to admit that he might be what he termed a 'bad screen-tester' and that seemed to be the case when, practically broke, he met director Emmerich and his co-producer Dean Devlin for the screen-test for *The Patriot*: 'I was hungry at times; it was my last hope. If I didn't get the part, I was going to go back home. I had nothing: no money, no nothing... At one point, I didn't even want to read the script and go in and meet with them. I had come so close to so many great projects that I just had the rub taken out of me. But I went in anyway and read for the director, Roland Emmerich, and the producer Dean Devlin and some other people.

'I had two scenes to read and was halfway through the second scene and just stopped. I said, "I'm sorry, this is shit; I'm wasting your time. But, more important, I'm wasting mine." I was so in the dumps, I just didn't give a shit. I stood up and walked out.' He added, 'I wasn't comfortable being there; I wasn't comfy in my own skin. It had been a long and hard year. I was dead broke, I was starving. So I left. I walked down the hallway with my tail between my legs and my head sunk. I was really nervous, but you know, I came back because I guess they were curious. I figured I had blown my last chance and I was tired from the whole year and I didn't feel like taking it to a place where I'd almost get the part and then see it go to someone else. That's why I left. But Roland and Dean must have liked something about me; either that, or they were curious about what kind of fool would walk out on an audition like that. When I went back, I thought, "Oh God, now I've really got to prove to them that I wasn't in the right head space."'

Mel Gibson, who'd been hiding in the wings, was then

hauled in next to Heath and Emmerich told the pair to try and look like father and son: 'So I desperately tried to look at Mel and see if I could make my face look like his. They said, "Turn profile, walk together, look at each other, turn," you know, it was silly. And then that was every day for three weeks, it was like, "Next day, tomorrow, I promise you, tomorrow we're going to find out. It has to be tomorrow." For three weeks, my life went on hold. And then I found out I got it, I'd got the part!' Of the few parts he had coveted during this laid-back spell in Los Angeles, Gabriel was the one he wanted most: 'He had depth to him, and an arc. He travelled somewhere, which is always so interesting.'

Devlin admitted he and Emmerich were intrigued. 'The thing about Heath is that he has the one quality that's hard to find in most young actors and that's the quality of being a man,' he said. 'Most 21-year-olds still feel like boys.' Emmerich too realised Heath possessed that something special that shines through on the screen: 'When he walked in the office everybody was kind of immediately straightening up and saying, "Who is this guy?" And he has quite an effect on women. Dean and I had a lot of women in the company. There was this thing there that all the women were rooting for Heath.'

If that audition was fraught, his first day of the four-month shooting of the $100 million epic in early autumn 1999 in South Carolina wasn't much of an improvement: he described his first day's work as 'hopeless.' As he explained: 'I hadn't been in front of a camera in a year and I'm facing Mel Gibson. It was very exciting, but I never really let anything get me too worked up until I got on set. I had about four months before shooting to let it sink in, but it never really sank in until the first time I sat down, looked into Mel's eyes and heard "Action!" and "Cut!" Then I started to shake. I went to Dean and said, "You've got to understand I'm freaked out." I was delusional.'

Even director Emmerich was forced to admit, 'I think Heath went home that first day a nervous wreck, he was so disappointed in himself. But he was actually pretty good that day, although you wouldn't be able to tell him that.' He added, 'You could see that he had a reverence for Mel because Mel is so big in Australia.'

Heath confessed, 'It was the first time I had to do an American accent; I hadn't done one before, I was really freaked out. And I went into it. I had a dialogue coach for like a week, and I got it kinda there. And then when I got on the set, for about the first three weeks I felt like I was just doing an accent, I wasn't acting. I was just so conscious of listening to my voice, making sure that it sounded American, that I didn't feel like I was acting.'

Fortunately the influence of having a man like Mel Gibson – a character who had a wealth of experience – was to have a beneficial effect: 'It was a real learning curve. I guess I was really nervous at first because it was such a big picture, and it was Mel Gibson. He's like my hero – our hero in Australia, for sure.

'But he put me at ease straightaway because he's such a lovely bloke, a really lovely guy. He's a gentleman. I didn't feel like I had to go in there and stand my ground. It wasn't like going into a boxing ring. I learned so much from him and a lot of it is sub-textual. I mean, what I did learn? And what I will share with you? I guess he really taught me a lot about just relaxing. Relaxing in the newfound position that I am, like socially and professionally.'

Gibson put the young Australian at ease: 'and then I just soaked up as much information as I could. Mel is a lovely, lovely man, and that's surprising because I know not everyone in his position is as friendly as he is. On the set, he's very much about relaxing. Keeping his head clear and not over-concentrating, keeping things fresh, keeping things happy and light – and humorous. And being that way in life. Because Mel, he walks to the beat of life. He really does, in such a wonderful, wonderful way. And I was honoured and extremely lucky, I guess, to have him as the first big blockbuster actor that I get to work with.'

He added, 'It took me about a week and then I relaxed. Mel's always joking; he's very light-hearted all the time. It was never a tense shoot. I soaked up as much information as I could. Mel is a lovely, lovely man, and that's surprising because I know not everyone in his position is as friendly as he is. It was kind of like we just knew how it was gonna be played. And we got along well from go. And we were mates and buddies, and then I guess it just wasn't that hard to translate it into a father-son relationship onscreen. The film's similar to what I went through with my father, getting to an age where you feel you had your own opinions and rules in life, taking off, doing it the hard way and not listening to what he has to say.'

After getting over his 'I'm working with a superstar' nerves, Ledger found there was a lot to learn from Gibson, to whom he had already been favourably compared: 'In so many ways I've learnt so many things from this guy,' he said. 'Most are unspoken and sub-textual, but we've spoken about how to deal with different pressures. He just showed me, in a way, how to keep yourself normal and sane, remain a normal guy and not let it take you to another planet. He's very good at that. After one day I saw that Mel was super-relaxed – then it was a walk in the park.'

Gibson put it more succinctly: 'He's more mature than I was at that age; he seems more worldly, seems to know his way around. He's incredibly quick. I recall how s**t-scared he was when we first started, but we joked around as guys do and before long, he fitted in perfectly.'

Movie-talk had it that Heath and Ryan Phillippe had been in the running for the role and Gibson confirmed it was a neck-and-neck affair, although he has never named the other actor involved. 'At first Roland wanted me to decide, but I couldn't,' Gibson said. 'So I told him that he was the director. He should make the decision, and I would be happy with it. And I was. Heath possesses an unlikely combination: he has incredible presence, yet he has no f***ing pretensions. He's much more grounded than I was at that age, when it all started happening for me. I think he'll handle it better than I did.'

One of the key elements of the film is Heath's character's desire to fight the British against the wishes of his father. He was able to come up with a stunningly simple example of a modern-day similar situation: 'Gabriel has been playing football all his life and he has an opportunity to go to the Super Bowl, but his father decides he shouldn't go,' he said in a magazine interview. 'And he can't understand because all his friends are going, so he takes off to play. It's the right thing to do but he learns the hard way.'

He also had some learning to do, primarily about the background and the events of the American War of Independence: 'I just knew the bare basics about George Washington and the idea of a new land fighting for independence. Luckily most of the facts I needed to know were in the screenplay although I also read a few books.' He also had to get accustomed to the military mood of the film – basically hand-to-hand fighting combined with shooting at your enemy from close range – and, on the DVD of the film, he said, 'The militia men were crazy, brutal and passion-driven. They had passion in their bellies – and they won because of that.' All that from a young man who, it must be remembered, had emphatically rejected joining the Cadet Corps at school.

Perhaps he should have acquired some skills when it came to handling guns as he might then have avoided an accident while filming: 'It's always fun with this job because you get to learn all these crazy little skills. I mean, when am I ever going to fire a musket again? And we did fire them. We set little bottles up on the hill and shot at them.' Indeed, his index finger got stuck against his gun's flint rock, essential in firing a musket. 'It was my first set of stitches. The worst thing about it was that the rock was layered with gunpowder that jammed into my wound so I was screaming like a baby. They took me to the hospital, gutted it out and stitched it up. I went straight back to work. They only gave me, like, three stitches, but I wanted five because I'd made such a fuss and I wanted to go back and say, "At least I had five stitches!"'

The Patriot was released in the summer of 2000 and at its première Heath said, 'I was shaking, crying and smiling, everything. I was really happy and proud of it.' As part of the promotion, he was interviewed by *Newsweek* magazine, who interestingly described him as 'frank and polite but comes within millimetres of being too cool for school. He arrives for lunch, looking like an 80s pop star: sleeveless red T shirt, green jeans, a Dolce & Gabbana leather jacket and a wide, black leather bracelet. Ledger is a Camel-smoker in a non-smoking building, and so he's jittery. He's constantly stretching, leaning back in his chair, folding and unfolding his napkin.' And so it goes on... What the interview did was to allow Heath to expand on the reason why he suddenly upped and left Australia for LA after the success of *Roar* – and it wasn't just for work.

'Ironically, it was a *Braveheart* rip-off,' he said, talking about the series. 'It was shot beautifully, and the script was half-decent. But by the fifth episode the ratings weren't going well, and all of a sudden sea sprites in bikinis were popping up. When the show was cancelled, I was in love and really, I followed a girl back to LA.' A reference no doubt to Lisa Zane, the woman he had become close to during the series' filming.

He also quickly developed a realistic assessment of the fame and whether or not it had changed him. As he told one interviewer, 'No, it just changes everyone else. It's strange, man. It's invading, intruding. It's yin and yang, it all balances out.' And being hailed as a massive sex-symbol didn't faze him either. 'I really, believe it or not, rarely sit around thinking about it. I guess there's a particular type who would, but I don't.'

Questions such as that formed part of many interviews that Heath gave about the film – and although the movie succeeded at the box-office it still needed all the help it could get. Reviews had not been over-critical, but they had by no means been unanimous in their praise. The carping over historical inaccuracies may not have helped – 'The Patriot is to history what Godzilla was to biology', said one historian – while some reviewers felt it was all a bit too predictable and indeed gory. Comparisons with The Last of the Mohicans didn't help either, although it must be said that Heath's performance escaped the sniping. In fact, the reviewers were generally more than favourable when it came to assessing his contribution to the film. He could be more than satisfied with his step up the ladder.

What didn't help was that the movie was released at the same time as the hugely popular Perfect Storm with George Clooney, while younger audiences were tempted by the attractions of Scary Movie or the extravagances of X-Men. The film world being what it is, even as The Patriot was prepared for release, Heath was busy on his next project, A Knight's Tale, being filmed in Prague. The cuttings libraries of the newspaper world were already starting to fill with references to the rangy young Western Australian, but they were mainly linked to his films and the interviews he gave to coincide with them. That summer, however, he was to depart from the film pages and move to the gossip columns and newspages as he became a real-life heart-throb.

So it was that when Heath decided to enjoy the night-life of the romantic Czech capital with a glamorous companion it was only a short time before news of his exploits began to leak out – especially as the woman alongside him was a film star too. Heather Graham had key roles in two of the most successful films of recent years. The 1997 film *Boogie Nights* was an examination of the Californian porn industry that was both a critical and box-office success, providing a boost to the slumbering career of Burt Reynolds and an aid to the rising success of William H Macey, Philip Seymour Hoffman and Mark Wahlberg. Graham had the major role of Brandy 'Rollergirl', a porn starlet. She also played Felicity Shagwell in the hilarious Mike Myers' spoof *Austin Powers: The Spy Who Shagged Me*. Like Heath she was filming in Prague – the city was a favourite with film-makers for the medieval feel of its architecture – and they were reported to be sharing candlelit dinners every night. Heath was 21, Heather aged 30. Heath and Heather... the names seemed to go together well.

CHAPTER 5

A STAR IS BORN

This time there was no big star to hide behind, no Mel Gibson to carry the strain; no safety net of it being an Australian film that was not expected to have an impact world-wide or the camouflage of being one of a large cast, as in *10 Things*.

A Knight's Tale was a full-blown 'biggie', a blockbuster that cost a fortune to make, which it needed to recoup – and more – if those associated with it were to carry on up the ladder of film success rather than slither down it.

And Heath Ledger was the star.

His was the name at the top of the cast list, his was the face staring down from countless posters – something he later confessed he had nothing to do with, which had 'horrified' him when he saw it. He would be doing the interviews that would promote the film, never a task he enjoyed, and so it was his task to encourage cinema-goers to part with their hard-earned money.

The reasoning was simple. In the way that football stars don't decide on their transfer fees when moving from one side to another, so actors – certainly not 21-year-old actors – are not the final arbiters of what film they will actually star in and how big the budget will be. Certainly they can refuse a role and Heath had already done that in the past but he wasn't the one who singled himself out to play the main role in *A Knight's Tale* – others did that for him. And it was obvious he felt that pressure. Executives at Columbia Pictures had already seen the early *Patriot* footage and realised from watching it that he had that special 'something' that could carry a film. 'From the time I read the *A Knight's Tale* script, he was always the person that we wanted,' said studio chairman Amy Pascal. 'We offer him everything,' was the pronouncement from the woman who came to be known as 'The Most Powerful Woman in Hollywood'.

A Knight's Tale lay in the future, however, when Heath met director Brian Helgeland at Los Angeles airport when he was heading home to Australia during a two-week break during filming for *The Patriot*. The director noticed a large leather case at the actor's feet and inside it was a didgeridoo, the aboriginal Australian wind instrument. Here, Helgeland takes up the tale: 'I said, "Can you play it?" and he said, "Yeah, I wouldn't be hauling it around if I couldn't play it."' He added, 'The irony is that every 20-year-old actor you meet carries a guitar with them. You say, "Can you play it?" and they say, "Well, not really." Or "I'm taking lessons," that kind of thing. That was the moment when I realised, I've got this period movie I'm trying to contemporise and here's this contemporary person playing an ancient instrument; it was just a good match.'

Heath, not surprisingly, also remembers the meeting well: 'I was flying out to take a holiday back home and Brian was flying in from some trip or other and we were both dog-tired and he was certainly jet-lagged... and the meeting wasn't exactly sparking along. To keep the conversation going, Brian asked me what I had in a long leather case. I opened it up, took out my didgeridoo and gave him a blast on that. I must have made something of an impression... I am just terrible at auditions, you know. I don't get any better, either. I'm aware of the fact that I'm being tested and judged, and I just crumple up and get nervous. My voice never comes out right and the nerves take over. Come to think of it, I might take the didgeridoo along to all my forthcoming auditions! I also think that I was helped by the curiosity that a lot of Americans have about anyone from a different society that comes to Hollywood. Why does that happen? But it does, thank God!'

It wasn't just the didgeridoo that impressed the director, however. Helgeland's assessment was: 'Heath doesn't seem to be of his generation.' Perhaps that helped him decide he was the ideal man for the role in his highly unusual take on medieval jousting in the 1370s. 'I needed kind of a young movie star for the part,' the director said. 'To me, a movie star, more than anything, is very self-possessed and there's

a very strong sense of who that person is, besides the
character they're playing. That self-possession is very hard
to find in a young person at all, never mind a young actor.
Usually, they're still trying to figure out who they are when
they're 20 and 21 years old. That's why I think movie stars
don't become apparent until they're 30 or 35 generally. Of
all the actors I met, Heath seemed to have that kind of
quality. He's playing William Thatcher. But it's also Heath
up on the screen, which seemed important to the story as
far as identity and all that kind of thing; he was very strong
that way.'

If Heath needed any convincing that he was now
definitely on the A-list, it must have come with the
combination of a $50 million budget and a director of
Helgeland's calibre, who had already directed Mel Gibson
in *Payback* and earned an Oscar for his screenplay for the
brilliant *L.A. Confidential*, starring two Down Under
actors, Russell Crowe and Guy Pierce. Intriguingly, he also
won a Razzie (the 'Oscars' for bad work) in the same year
for his script on the Kevin Costner disaster *The Postman* –
and he turned up to collect his award, one of the few
winners ever to have the nerve or the sense of humour to
do so.

That humorous view of life was to surface again in *A
Knight's Tale*, which he wrote as well as directed. But not
for him a predictable jousting romp, with maidens' hearts
a-fluttering and the odd swordfight to liven up the
proceedings. Instead he peppered it with classic rock
songs such as Queen's 'We Will Rock You', 'Golden

Years' by David Bowie and Thin Lizzy's 'The Boys Are Back in Town'. The crowds at the jousts were to react not with polite applause and the genteel waving of a perfumed handkerchief; instead they rose in Mexican waves of approval.

Helgeland was to joke that he chose 1970s music and hairstyles for the movie because 'the seventies are always the same,' regardless of century. And he justified his use of music by speculating that even during the 1370s, people in the main characters' age group would have enjoyed newer, more contemporary music than something that had been around since their great-grandparents were young. So he chose music that would affect the audience the same way late-1300s music might have moved the youth of the 1370s. It was his way of using this extremely stylised film to bring the Middle Ages to the audience rather than force the audience back to the Middle Ages.

Heath's role was the central one and he played William Thatcher, a young squire, who, after the death of his knight Sir Ector joins the jousting circuit, an act, according to the film anyway, forbidden to those not of noble birth.

Under the somewhat over-the-top name of Sir Ulrich von Lichenstein, he travelled around Europe accompanied by his fellow squires, Wat and Roland, and his well spoken herald, Geoffrey Chaucer. Chaucer went on to write *The Canterbury Tales* and the premise of Heath's movie is that this is what he got up to before penning his masterpiece, the first story of which was called 'The Knight's Tale'.

Thatcher falls in love with Jocelyn, played by Hawaiian-born Shannyn Sossamon, who was making her film debut, having been discovered at Jake and Gwyneth Paltrow's joint birthday party, where she was the DJ. Thatcher also becomes a fierce rival of Count Adhemar of Anjou (Rufus Sewell), the villain of the piece.

All good fun, and Heath seemed to reflect that mood when he said filming was 'light and happy', adding, 'It's fun to kick up your heels every now and then.' As for the action-adventure aspect, his verdict was, 'It just seems like I can't get off a horse – I'm on a horse in every bloody movie I've done! I'm on a horse in *The Patriot*, and I'm on a horse in *Knight's Tale*, and next I'm on a camel!' (Referring to his upcoming appearance in *The Four Feathers*.) Yet even in this apparently light-hearted mood he was still able to analyse exactly what made his character tick: 'It's an identity crisis for this character because he thinks that to achieve something in life he has to be at a certain status. He doesn't want to be nothing and nothing is a peasant and a squire. So he goes out to discover that.'

In case that sounded all too serious, he was also at pains to point out what appealed to him in the role and the film in general: 'I really loved it. It was so well written; it really did have everything – the comedy was written really well. The drama was driven, the action sounded out of this world. I was curious how they were going to pull that off. From the moment I heard the concept, I really dug it. When I read the first page of the script and it said the film opens with the song, "We Will Rock You," I thought to myself, "Oh God, what are they trying for here? This is really risky!" But the more I read on, I began to realise the beauty of it. It gave licence and room to play without being restricted by historical facts; it blasted that out. It was like, here's some rock'n'roll, so we're not going to be tied down to having to be historically correct. We're making a movie, just a movie, a fairy tale.'

It was just as well that he was enjoying the filming because he had a four-month stay in Prague while the movie was being made. Halfway through, he reflected: 'I lived in Los Angeles for two years. I have a storage unit here and a car, and that's my home. I've been in Prague now for two months, with another two months there before I go to Morocco for four months. So I don't live anywhere at all. I'm like a gypsy, I guess. It's fun; I just live out of my bags.'

Despite being on horseback for much of the filming, he was still missing similar, but much less pressured pleasures back in Los Angeles: 'I used to go riding with an Australian friend of mine. He'd been out here for a while and somehow he got a job at a horse ranch as a tour guide. And they'd shut down every night around 6 or 7 and we'd go out there and grab the horses and ride all through the night to the observatory.' Athletic and mobile as Heath undoubtedly was, stuntmen still had to be used for some of his scenes: 'All the jousting – I obviously didn't take any hits or hit anyone, it was just way too dangerous. The stunt guys did that for us. But all the sword fights were me.'

The first action sequence of two knights jousting is, in reality, footage of Heath's stunt double in an accident.

During filming of a later scene, the lance of the stunt double's opponent hit the double in the head. He fell to the ground unconscious. Even more unusual was the incident where the star knocked the director's teeth out – not customary in film-making. Heath and Helgeland were demonstrating a jousting move when Heath accidentally struck the director with a broomstick. The damage was so bad it was several months before it could be properly repaired.

On screen the safety measures were thankfully much better as the stem of every lance used was scored so that it would snap under virtually any impact, no matter how slight, and would break easily. The tips were made of hollowed-out balsa wood, filled with balsa chippings, sawdust and uncooked pasta – to make the impact all the more realistic. Over 1,000 lances ended up being used during filming. One day, 8 of them were needed on set but they broke with such rapidity that 44 were used in that day alone.

It was obvious during the making of the film that Heath was heading for stardom. He even merited one of the unmistakable signs of impending fame, a cover story for *Vanity Fair* in which he looked relaxed and smiling in the bright sunlight, leaning nonchalantly against a wall in Bruce Weber's photograph, his curly, unkempt fair hair flopping, brown eyes sparkling. Clothed in a workman's white vest above a pair of faded jeans, it was an image of a remarkably poised and calm young man. Yes, it was posed, but in no way was it an artificial languidness; it all seemed so natural.

One night after filming had stopped for the day, he gave the magazine's writer, Kevin Sessums, an insight into his views on life and his career, including an explanation of why he had never bothered to have an acting lesson: 'I don't have a method to my madness. For me, acting is more about self-exploration,' he said. 'I've learned a lot about myself in order to learn about the craft. How many kings can you find to play a king? You can't find them. When I act, I look at it as if I'm a mixing board in a sound studio: the pattern on the board is me. When I play a character, I go, "I'll turn these knobs down and these ones up." But in order to do that I have to know myself; I have to know myself like an instrument – I'm just a saxophone. I've always been very big on self-exploration and answering my own questions. For so many, it's hell growing up but I guess I'm blessed: I've really enjoyed it. I don't let a lot get to me, I really don't. As I keep saying, I break everything down, everything. I look up at the stars and go, "There's no explanation for us to be here." When anything is blocking my head or there's worry in my life, I just – whoosh! – go sit on Mars or something and look back here at Earth. All you can see is this tiny speck; you don't see the fear, you don't see the pain, you don't see the movie industry, you don't see this interview, you don't see thought... It's just one solid speck. Then nothing really matters, it just doesn't.'

In the background he would play music from another era, eerily that of Janis Joplin and Jim Morrison of The Doors, two singers who died far too young after living life in rock's fast lane. These were strange words indeed from a film star for they are the ones, the very word 'star' implies it, who often feel we should all gaze at in awe, yet Heath was placing himself as a very small fragment of the universe. Perhaps that unusual take on life was in some way influenced by his blossoming relationship with Heather Graham, who he met in the Fromin nightclub in Prague. She was filming *From Hell* in the Czech capital – she co-starred alongside Johnny Depp – at the same time as Heath, and the attraction between the two was instant.

A decade his senior, her upbringing had been as severe and strict as Heath's had been laid-back and Australian super-cool. Graham was born in Milwaukee, Wisconsin, to devout Catholic parents although her family later settled in Virginia and then finally moved to the suburban Agoura Hills in California. Her mother was a schoolteacher – like Heath's – who later wrote children's books, but her father had a different lifestyle altogether: he was an FBI agent who worked on terrorism cases. 'He really didn't talk much about what he was doing. He was sworn to secrecy... although one time he came on the set of some film I was doing and told me, "That's not the way you put handcuffs on,"' she said.

It was a restrictive and religious upbringing and her parents even banned the innocuous and extremely popular television series *The Love Boat* from their home on the grounds that it featured premarital sex. The strictness of her upbringing was to contrast sharply with the free-spirited, and often unclothed, roles she went on to appear in. Indeed she was later to be critical of their attitudes admitting, 'I used to try to create the appearance of what people wanted me to be, especially for my parents. Maybe it's that whole WASP thing – that I came from that land of "blonde girls whose clothes always fit right", but I was never like that. As a kid, I was a total nerd. I always felt I was different, but I hid it until I felt more comfortable with people.'

She started drama lessons at 16 and was to graduate to the status she was enjoying when she first met Heath. The difference in their ages did not bother him at all. He had already lived with one older woman, Lisa Zane, and he summed up his feelings for Heather in this way: 'When you look someone in the eyes, and you see what you see, you don't think numbers, you don't think words, you just feel. Our relationship is based on trust – we have a mental devotion to each other.' Admitting there were benefits in dating an actress – 'I need someone who can understand my work' – he was nevertheless cautious about any long-term plans. Perhaps wary due to his childhood memories of his parents' divorce he said simply, 'I don't want to turn love into a contract.'

It was unusual for him to make any pronouncements on his private relationships, but he allowed some more information into the public domain when he told Australia's *Herald-Sun* about his affection for Heather – as well as buying and decorating himself a home in Hollywood. He said, 'Nothing in my personal circle has changed... just everything else around it. That doesn't really bother me. Fame has not reached a point yet where I can't go out and enjoy myself with my mates. To tell you the truth, I have been working non-stop for 18 months... six-day weeks. I have not really had time to notice how my life might have changed. Acting is a job, I love it, but it is just a job. You still have to eat, pay the bills.

'She is my muse,' he added (referring, of course, to Heather) and, 'It's strange owning a house. I have virtually been living out of bags for five years while I have been on the road. But all of a sudden, I have got a place and it's on paper saying this is where you live, this is your home; it is a bit restrictive. It's kind of funny because I still don't feel like I have any possessions. It's hard to believe...' And the making of *A Knight's Tale* sounded as though it was an upbeat four months, even without meeting Graham: 'It was a lot of fun. I made very good friends with these people... that friendship transcends on screen, a bunch of people who fell in love with one another. I got a chance to fight, dance, sing – I wasn't improvising; it was in the script. I like dancing and singing. I would love to do a musical one day. This has certainly sparked my interest.

'The story wasn't restricted by saying it was historically correct. The floodgates were opened with the contemporary music. It had a more modern vision.'

Despite the anti-military sentiments he had expressed at school, Heath didn't find any contradiction in playing combative roles in both *The Patriot* and *A Knight's Tale*: 'Ultimately I am just portraying a character. It is not about me getting up there and telling the audience this is what I believe in. I am up there telling a story. If I play an axe murderer, it doesn't mean I am going to go out there and chop someone's head off.'

Despite the obvious good times he had filming *A Knight's Tale*, it wasn't without its physical drawbacks, especially when it came to wearing the heavy armour in which he spent much of the film: 'It was hot, it was heavy, it was sweaty. It was also itchy. I spent most of the time rubbing myself up against the nearest tree.' Nevertheless he pointed out: 'On and off screen, it was a ball. All the horse-riding, jousting and sword-fighting was great. But as soon as I sat down with Brian, I'd known it was going to be fun. I could tell he was planning a wonderful playground for us all.

'With something like *Knight's Tale* though they are adventure fantasies, at least the characters I play are pretty three-dimensional. They have a history to them, a past and a bit of truth to them – which I like. In fact, I can identify with William Thatcher because both he and I want to feel equal to society. He wants to be up there with the aristocracy – not perhaps to be one of them, but to be on equal terms with them and have the same opportunities. I've always wanted to stomp on that "them and us" thing, too. He wants to be noble – but from the inside. His nobility comes from within, and that's true of me too – I wish.'

The film avoided the temptation of using computer-generated images, opting instead for re-creating as accurately as possible a 14th-century feel. 'What you see on the screen is real,' he emphasised. 'We had that luxury of a month for rehearsals that bonded us, and besides our filming in the Czech countryside exteriors were constructed on a back-lot at the historic Barrandov Studios, where we headquartered. The area was larger than two football fields, and it included the sets you see of medieval London, Rouen and a jousting field. Also, an ice arena on the Vtalva River island in the heart of Prague became the setting for our enormous banquet hall where we perform our dances, as well as the interiors of the French cathedrals, Rouen and Notre Dame.'

He added that their jousting trainers came from Las Vegas: 'We worked with such specialists as a lance-master and a horse-master, armourers, weapons' handlers, leather workers, stunt wizards and exotic animal handlers. The lances in one scene totalled more than 1,000. As for the horsemanship, I've been comfortable in the saddle for a number of years.' Production crews scoured the Czech Republic for the rare Kladruby horses – giant animals with lineage dating back more than 700 years, when they pulled royal carriages or served as the medieval equivalent of tanks.

Heath was realistic enough to know his physical limitations. Superbly fit and lean as he was, he was fully aware that if he was transported back by some kind of magic to the 14th century then it would be all too much for him to cope with such a lifestyle: 'I wouldn't survive a f***ing week! I'd be hopeless – actually, a week? I'd be dead within the hour! I think that it's every man for every hour – William wouldn't have survived in the world of today, and I wouldn't have survived back then. But the nice thing about the script was that it made these guys [his co-stars Mark Addy, Rufus Sewell and James Purefoy] all really contemporary people with contemporary emotions. OK, I researched a bit about the sport of jousting, and how it was done, but then I relied on what I know and what I feel. All I can tell you is that that armour we had to wear was hot – the temperatures out in Prague were around 40°C, and you could feel the stuff sizzling on your flesh. The guys in the crew were always coming over and pouring bottles of Evian water between the gaps in the metal to cool us down.'

Actors and crew partied pretty hard in Prague, but it wasn't too surprising as that type of action had been the order of the day from the very start. Brian Helgeland actually assembled the majority of his cast four weeks ahead of the main shooting. 'Then he got us pissed for a month,' said Heath, with very un-movie star-like frankness. 'We had precisely one table reading, at which we were all blind-drunk. But that was a smart move because this movie is really about friendship. By the end of that month, we really, really liked each other.'

The famous posters, with Heath's handsome face glaring massively out from them, weren't quite so much to his liking, for now-familiar reasons: 'When I saw the poster for the movie I was pretty freaked; I got really nervous. I think I started shaking. The film is an ensemble piece, and there's just my great, big mug. Sure, the story is based around this knight's character, but it's about a group of people. It's an ensemble piece – it always was... It was like, f**k! I've done all this work, but ultimately, these guys are making decisions that could either really make or break my career. And it's out of my hands, I'm just doing what I've always done – being an actor. Now I'm being made into a "star", a product, and it's out of my control.

'Ultimately, the guys who run the studios probably don't even see the movies. It's all about the figures, not how good the movies are. Of course, they don't give a shit about my personal life. They like to take a kid like me and say, "Let's slick his hair, put him in a suit and mould him into a superstar, so he can become this and that for us." But I'll surprise them. My parents couldn't change me, so there's no way I'm going to let these guys.'

More and more, he had to deal with comparisons with that icon of Australian cinema, Mel Gibson. 'I never expect anything like that,' he told one interviewer. 'It's an honour to have your name next to his, anyway. It's strange, they seem to call every Australian actor who's up and coming the next Mel Gibson – there's like six of us.'

Helgeland had a simple take on it: 'People say to me that he's the next Mel Gibson, I tell them, "No, he's the next Errol Flynn."' The reference to the Tasmanian-born actor who went on to become one of the biggest stars Hollywood has ever seen was yet another glowing tribute.

And when *A Knight's Tale* opened, the bandwagon kept rolling on. First of all, the critics, by and large, were impressed. The film also gave sub-editors on countless newspapers the chance to roll out the puns with headlines such as: 'Aussie Heath is Joust the Ticket,' 'Joust Right for a Fun Knight Out' and 'It's Joust a Good Knight Out.' Oh dear! There were countless others like that, but at least the vast majority were favourable, of both the film in general and Heath in particular.

Even newspapers such as the London-based *Guardian* fell under its spell – and that of its leading man: 'This is a deeply silly film. It deserves a special Silly Oscar of its own. It has the silliest lines, the silliest set-pieces, the silliest performances of anything I can ever remember seeing. And yet I came out of the cinema with a great big grin on my face. It's somehow very entertaining and its bizarre, in-your-face anachronisms are carried off with such insouciance, such cheerful effrontery, that you can't help indulging them... Hollywood's hunk of the moment, Heath Ledger, plays William Thatcher: that surname perhaps a clue to his entrepreneurialism and upward social mobility. He is a humble but ambitious squire in medieval days, who seizes his moment of destiny when his knight keels over and dies just before a big contest. (With his tousled, beach-blond hair, Ledger is actually a pretty good approximation of Chaucer's Squire: "A lovyere and a lusty bacheler")...'

A pretty erudite summary of Heath's charm and impact, but it was reflected in much more matter-of-fact manner by cinema audiences drawn to the film by its unusual take on what could easily have been a clichéd Hollywood format – and Heath's presence. As the posters promised, 'He Will Rock You'.

Heath, as always, remained unfazed: 'This hype about me wasn't a natural thing that started from people seeing my movies. It was Columbia seeing *The Patriot* and saying, "Oh, we can put this kid in this next movie. Let's pump him in this movie and let's create him in the next one, let's create a f***ing star so we can sell this movie and rake in the bucks!"'

Amy Pascal of Columbia Pictures, the woman who earmarked Heath for the starring role, was much more placatory: 'I don't see him as a product. He's at a time where he's having to sell a movie that is mostly on his back, which is a scary thing the first time you do it.' Part of the studio's efforts to push the film involved asking Ledger to embark on a 12-city North American promotional tour, which he eventually scaled down as he felt it was too demanding.

And as if to reiterate that his attitude to the projects he accepted or declined was governed by their quality rather than 'blockbuster' rating, he even passed on the lead role in *Spider-Man*. The part eventually went to Tobey Maguire and made him an international star. You could almost sense the same feeling in his bones that he had possessed during that 'lull' in Los Angeles when he binned the teen-movie projects, when he said: 'I've no regrets about *Spider-Man*. I just wasn't interested in comic books, I have never read them; I have never been a big fan of them. I thought it would be so much fun to make but I just didn't have the enthusiasm for it. I just didn't, I knew I would be doing it just to do it. That is not fun. I just don't care for comics, never have. Never cared for Spider-Man. It would have been stealing someone else's dream.'

He was to add at a later stage in his career: 'I hadn't at that point, and still haven't, secured a position as an actor who can act. I've done some crappy s**t and I haven't showcased myself yet. It would have been a lot harder to go from being Spider-Man on every poster to getting nitty-gritty little roles on independent movies with really good stories, good characters, good writing... I think it's a lot harder to go the other way. Whereas, if you can prove yourself and do the hard yards and pump out some performance, and create something solid in you first and foremost then you can afford to do that.'

He may not have been destined to wear the comic book hero's famous costume, but this didn't prevent his army of fans, both male and female, from growing. As always, he took it characteristically in his stride. Of the women he simply said, 'That's cool.' And as far as the male admirers went, 'I have no problem with that at all. It's nice, but I don't care. It's not something that I think about. All of that – the fan base, the websites, people who admire me in that way – well, it's all outside my own small world, and certainly it's outside my little circle of friends.'

He didn't have too much time to ponder on his 'metrosexual' appeal as he would soon be learning to ride the camel that he had recently spoken of. No sooner had *A Knight's Tale* finished in the Czech Republic than Heath was packing those bags of his again and heading for Morocco.

CHAPTER 6

HEATH, HEATHER AND THE SPLIT

It would be hard to think of a more 'English' story than *The Four Feathers*. Not just because of the genteel, upper-class late Victorian England setting, but also the moral message of honour, friendship, bravery and decency redolent of a time and attitude long gone.

The life story of the author of the original novel *The Four Feathers*, Alfred Edward Woodley Mason, almost reads like a stiff upper-lip parody of such an era. Educated at Dulwich College in south London and then Trinity College, Oxford, he was briefly a Liberal Member of Parliament and served in the Manchester Regiment during World War I – the war to end all wars – and rose to the rank of Major. As well as *The Four Feathers*, his works included *Fire Over England* (1937) and *The Prisoner in the Opal* (1929), titles that oozed a sense of imperialism and empire. By the time of his death in 1948 *The Four Feathers* had already been filmed four times, the first two versions being for the silent screen and Heath's film was to be the seventh time the story was committed to celluloid.

The reason was simple: as well as the human traits it explored, its narrative was ripe for the big screen, bursting as it was with military action, exotic settings and with a strong romantic theme running through. This was a genuine 'ripping yarn' with a tear-jerking love story woven into it. Set in 1884, Harry Feversham (Heath) is a young officer-in-training in the British Army, soon to graduate and expected to be shipped off to the Sudan, where the Army is fighting Muslim insurgents who are attempting to overturn English colonial rule. Feversham, however, has developed serious doubts about his future and on the eve of his departure, he resigns his commission. In response, his best friend and fellow officer Jack Durrance (played by Wes Bentley) presents him with a symbol of cowardice – a white feather – and two of his classmates follow suit. Harry's fiancée Ethne Eustace, portrayed by Kate Hudson, gives him a fourth white feather shortly before breaking off their engagement.

Humiliated, he attempts to win back his honour and the respect of his family and friends by secretly becoming an undercover operative in the Sudan. There, he makes friends with a local man sympathetic to the British cause who proves to be a valuable source of insider information and advice on how to blend with the rebels. Meanwhile, Durrance is briefly ordered back to England to help recruit new soldiers for the colonial forces and he takes the opportunity to begin wooing Eustace.

Durrance is later blinded (but rescued by Harry). Both Ethne and Jack think Harry is dead and so they become engaged. In reality he is rescuing his other two friends from imprisonment, showing astonishing courage and endurance on the way. The feathers are all eventually returned to him, proof that he is no longer considered a coward, and the course of true love runs smoothly after all. Great stuff and ripe for parody, yes, but it was also wonderful material for a sweeping adventure film. For Heath, it was a fantastic role as 'leading man' in the old-fashioned sense.

Shooting was scheduled to begin in Morocco in the autumn of 2000, a far cry from chilly Prague, and so he would be setting off on his travels again. This time his director was Shekhar Kapur, who had won international recognition for his film *Elizabeth*, about the life and loves of Queen Elizabeth I. The film had been nominated for seven Oscars and had also scooped up a clutch of BAFTAs, as well as bringing award after award for its leading player, Australian actress Cate Blanchett. Lahore-born Kapur, who divided his time between London and India, came from an acting background and he had started his career in Bollywood with films such as *Masooim* and *Mr. India*, which were critically acclaimed and hugely successful at the box office.

Many people thought *The Four Feathers*, with its overriding sense of the heroism and purpose of British colonialism, was a strange subject for Kapur to tackle but he explained it by saying that he was strongly drawn to one of the themes of the novel and wanted to focus on it in a version of the story that would be quite different from others that had been filmed before. 'When I read the novel, I was attracted to the theme of cowardice,' he said.

Although the book seemed to brand Heath's character a coward for not going to war, Kapur said he couldn't accept that idea and decided to approach the theme of cowardice from a different angle: 'Is an act of saying, "No, I won't go to war" an act of courage or an act of cowardice? It's easier to say "yes" whenever there is pressure, not just in a battle – this is what life is all about. Most of us find it easier to go with the flow. It's much more difficult to stop and think and say: "What is my choice? What is the hero? What is the nature of being the hero?" That's the main reason to make this film. *Four Feathers* is increasingly important now in a world that is telling you what to do all the time. You don't have time any more to ask yourself, "Who am I?" It's very relevant today.'

Warming to his theme, he continued, 'There was an acceptance of the idea that the Western world must go out and conquer other civilisations. It was your moral duty because the people in those places were heathens and they needed to be civilised. It was such a colonial story, I decided, why not subvert it? So I set out to make a very anti-colonial movie. When the colonists leave, they leave an artificial culture. When India and Pakistan were at a nuclear flash-point recently and the world was getting worried, nobody actually said it, but Britain created these two countries. My mother remembers when she was a girl, British soldiers coming and taking her father away. She remembers her brother coming and hiding a gun under her pillow; he was later shot dead. So I grew up believing that colonisation was the worst thing you could do to people. In a larger sense, Harry's struggle represents the battle between organisation and chaos – between East and West, Christianity and Islam – and the West's fundamental fear of being overwhelmed. Those facts are now so much in the forefront because of September 11th. I didn't predict them, but I knew that was where the world was heading.'

He was realistic enough to know that not everyone who saw the film would realise its depth, when he subsequently added at the Toronto Film Festival: 'The film on one plot level is just a plot but if you get carried by the subtext of the film there's a lot in there; it's a journey of a man from youth to wisdom. Ultimately, the external canvas of the film is just a journey of discovery of self. It's talking about structure and chaos – the structure of British society and the fear of the chaos of the East. Today, it's become the fear of the chaos of Islam. We have a civilisation [in the West] we can define, but what's attacking us is indefinable; it's chaotic.'

Heath's heroic character, 'sets out on the greatest journey of life, to find himself. Out of the chaos, he rebuilds himself. He comes not to structure but to harmony and wisdom.' The film was actually completed before the 9/11 attacks on New York but the director felt, 'the root causes of terror exist in colonisation' and that in the centuries leading up to the setting of the movie the British had no experience as 'a culture of grief; only a culture of triumph. *The Four Feathers* is a classic story, but also I saw the opportunity to use the epic scale to talk about these things.'

So much then for a simple *Boys Own* story, but regardless of whatever level the film was perceived as being on, Heath went through yet another fairly tortuous, and invariably almost truncated audition for the role which at one time was said to be destined for Jude Law.

He described it in this way: 'I had to put myself through the ringer. I spent eight hours one day with Shekhar and we shot about 15,000 feet of film. He really scrutinised me. There is a moment halfway through the audition when I was just going to stand up and walk out. I thought, "F**k this!" It was just way too intense. But then I had this vision of a little white feather turning up on my doorstep with a card from Shekhar,' he joked, 'so I stuck in there.' In a more serious vein he outlined his reasons for taking the part, the first being his admiration for his director's work, the second, simply, 'the role was amazing. It was such an epic journey of self-discovery. There is nothing written like that these days. I thought there was a hell of a lot of subtext underneath the story, and I was excited to fill that in.'

He also identified strongly with Harry's decision not to serve in the army: 'If I were called up, I'd take the feather. I went to a school that was slightly military based and they were teaching little kids how to fire semi-automatic weapons. I really didn't approve of that.' And then he added, 'Hopefully, we're all going to f***ing learn our lessons before the clowns – the people running the countries – start throwing nuclear weapons about. I think their brains are about the size of a pea, to tell you the truth.'

As with *A Knight's Tale*, horses played a key part in the filming: 'I had to do basic horse training again. No matter how well you can ride a horse, they always teach you how to trot again. I swear, at the beginning of every movie, they say, "Well, we don't know for sure that you can ride a horse, so we're going to put you through training. Now go on out there and trot." So I went out there and did a lap in a field, so then they said, "OK, he can ride a horse."' He continued, 'It's fun to balance out this film with action. There's so much emotional strain and stress throughout the whole movie. It was kind of refreshing to just get out there and scream and beat people up and jump on horses. It keeps it exciting.'

Not everyone was so laid-back about enacting scenes that were normally the preserve of a stuntman. One film insider at the time revealed, 'The insurers were having kittens because if anything had happened to him we would have been in deep trouble. And I don't know what the stuntmen thought – they charge per fall.' The previous year 4 extras on the film were injured after an accident during filming at Greenwich Naval College, London, when a horse reared and a carriage flipped over. Three people were taken to hospital and one man, with serious head injuries, was airlifted from the scene.

Vic Armstrong, whose stunt company worked on the film, admitted Heath had a natural aptitude for such scenes: 'It's very unusual for the stars to do stunts at that high level. He's a natural mover – he's really good. He's like a young Harrison Ford.'

The director, it seems, forgot to mention to studio execs that his star was taking such a risk: 'I said, "Heath, don't get killed." He said, "Shekhar, you've always told me it's in your destiny. I will die if it's God's will." It was very chancy, but then you know what? It's God's will. Movie studios don't understand God's will, but they are subject to God's will too, whether they like to believe that or not. At first we couldn't shoot the kind of action we wanted to.' He consulted with Heath in private and together they decided to do something extraordinary to give the film an unprecedented element of excitement in one battle scene.

But even to the director that element, running through a herd of galloping horses, sounded like too much: 'I told Heath: "You could get killed doing this." But he said, "OK, I can show how I die then." He's crazy. He is a particular kind of actor who has got an ability to open himself up and show it on the screen, representing not only the script but life itself. It was a great action scene, but later I got a letter from the film studio, saying that if I do this again, I can never work in Hollywood again!'

Heath, as ever, took a philosophical view: 'I didn't have to prepare physically, but I did have to prepare mentally for working in the desert. Just to get in that frame of mind of what I needed to do. Once you're out there, you become a product of your environment. You just kind of become immune to it. At the end of the day, I always cleaned right up before I left the make-up trailer. I made sure the beards were off and the wigs were off; that was the best part of the day for me.' And as for working with camels? 'It was OK. I really like camels a lot. I don't know what people have against them. I think they're great, delightful creatures.'

Perhaps his tongue was firmly in his cheek as he said that, for by the time the film opened, he was comfortable to admit, 'I'd be more than happy to stay off a horse for quite a while and I'd be happier still if I never rode a camel again.' If there were lighter moments on the set, once filming had finished for the day, Heath discovered that Morocco was very, very different from the loose, beer-drinking charms he had enjoyed so much in Prague: 'When you work with Shekhar Kapur it's a real commitment. I learnt so much from him but he took out so much. You have to devote yourself to him and if you do that, he will take you somewhere special. He's an extremely passionate film-maker. In Prague, everyone had their own little apartment and we would meet around the corner for coffee, you know. The apartments are gorgeous and it's a great little city. In Morocco, there was one hotel in the place where we were shooting and that was it, so we were stuck. That was my life for four months – in my hotel room by myself and there was nothing else beyond that. It was crazy.'

'Crazy' it might have been, but by the time shooting finished Heath had more than made up for that initial period of inactivity in Los Angeles. He had been working for 18 months without a break on 3 major films. It was time for a break and who better to take with him than the woman in his life at the time, Heather Graham? Never one to talk too publicly about his romances, he did let slip, 'I'm madly in love and deliriously happy' – but he didn't want to enlarge on that.

Soon afterwards, though, he did admit, 'All that craziness doesn't really affect the way Heather and I feel toward each other. You can't complicate that unless – well, I guess that it can [be], but it isn't. You know what? I don't read anything that gets written about us, so that helps a lot. We haven't had people [photographers] jumping out of bushes yet, but I know it's just a matter of time. Most of the time you don't even know they're there. Now that's the scary thing. It's really strange and invading, but I'm still working it all out. I try to not let it bother me; I really try and find the humour in all of it. And if I want to swim naked in my pool, I'm still going to do it. I certainly don't want to feel that I have to change everything in my life that I do to cater to them. I just won't let it happen.'

A combination of living in Los Angeles, buying a home there and filming in South Carolina, Prague and Morocco all conspired to make Heath feel like a man who lived out of a suitcase. Nevertheless, he had managed to buy a 2000 Land Rover Discovery and a 1970 Ford Mustang – a 'blokey' car is how he described it: 'It's a Muscle Car. I've never had a Muscle Car, never wanted one and then I drove this thing and my God, I just understood. It was like all of a sudden you feel like a real man; it was like riding a horse, you feel the engine under you.' During one article around this time, he showed his interviewer a fax received from his agent imploring him, no doubt light-heartedly, to 'call me, you bastard.'

His response was, 'I'm just not calling him. They want me to get a cell phone so they can hunt me down but I won't do that. I don't like cell phones – they kill moments. When I'm with my friends and I'm not working, we'll all be sitting around talking and everyone's relaxed and then all of a sudden it's like, brring brring. And everyone sits back while someone answers their phone. It just kills the moment, absolutely just shatters it. And I can't afford to lose those moments – I enjoy them too much.'

He was in need of a break so where better to travel with his new girlfriend than back to Australia to meet some family and friends? Before the journey, he admitted excitedly, 'I have a place here in LA, but it's not home; I don't think this place is anyone's home. The only reason that we're all here is work, it's a professional city. So that's why I'm so excited to be going back home to Perth. For the first time in five years, I'll be spending three weeks there doing nothing but having fun, and I'm really thrilled about that. I've been working straight for 18 months, 6-day weeks, so I think a break is in order.'

By this time he was no longer just 'Heath Ledger – Actor to Watch' but 'Movie Hero Heath Ledger – with his Film-star Girlfriend!' Any hopes of slipping in and out of the country like 'normal' people were now dashed. And it can't have lowered his profile that his name constantly appeared on lists of the 'handsomest men' and the words 'hunk' and 'hunky' seemed to be attached to virtually every article about him and review of every film in which he appeared. The influential *People* magazine even placed him in their list of 'The Sexiest Men Alive' in between Mel Gibson and, somewhat strangely, the television naturalist, the late Steve Irwin, best known for his wrestling with alligators, snakes and assorted deadly creatures.

By this time he had called Heather 'my muse' and she had referred to him as 'a great guy... I feel protective of him, so I don't want to say too much. But he's an incredible, amazing person, and I'm really lucky to know him.' She added: 'I just have to say that Heath is the greatest. He is an amazing person, incredible, and so Australians must be doing something right. He is just so relaxed and I feel like Australia must be like that... He's very talented and doing some really good films.' And what of the age difference? 'I just think you gotta go with who you are in love with, you know? We were having this discussion [on the set of a film she was in] about love at first sight. I believe you can see somebody and feel the possibility of love, but I've never met anyone and been in love with him that second. I think you meet somebody and feel that possibility and that excitement, and then kind of grow into it. It's better to fall in love and risk the pain and heartbreak of having it end than not take risks... there's no love without fear. You just have to get through that fear and go for it.'

As for Heath, he told *USA Today*: 'Heather is a wonderful, beautiful girl. I love her. She just makes me laugh.'

So it was that on 4 April 2001, his 22nd birthday, Heath and Heather flew into Sydney en route for Perth and attracted the full glare of the media. The trip did not get off to a particularly auspicious start in that Australian newspapers reported the Ledger party parked in an airport 'no-parking' area at Perth and made rude gestures to passers-by when this was pointed out. Hardly behaviour likely to start a riot, but it was indicative of the microscopic attention the couple would be coming under. Days later they were spotted kissing and cuddling in the gigantic swimming pool at the Burswood Resort Casino Hotel. According to a newspaper report they 'had eyes, arms and legs only for each other. They duck-dived, frolicked around the pool's giant boulders and on the water slide, laughing, hugging and kissing.'

If that didn't show how closely their every move would be followed, there was even an item a few days afterwards reporting on how they had visited an eatery in the Scarborough Beach area of Perth, which breathlessly told how the waitress who served them said that Heather ordered the big breakfast – although she only ate the eggs – while Heath stuck to muesli. And how they both drank freshly squeezed juice!

Meanwhile, Heath looked up old friends, slept in his old bed and even ate his mother's hunza pie – a vegetarian dish made of brown rice, eggs and cheese. Perhaps he even stocked up with Vegemite, which his family had been sending him in America. But there was no doubt the attention from the media and the public cast a shadow over his longed-for break. He remarked, 'I was really unprepared for it. Of all the places you wish to just stay the same, it's your home. You want that to be the same, and it wasn't. I couldn't do anything. It makes front-page news if you eat fettuccine on Tuesday. I came straight off working 18 months, and all this was bubbling up while I was working, so when I arrived – bang! – it had all changed.'

On another occasion he remarked: 'It's really strange. You can't really do anything. People know where you are eating and when and what, everything you are doing. They write it down. It's really sad for them. I think it's really sad of those people who are doing that but it's even sadder that people pay them to do that; it's a business. Your private life starts to become a public business.'

They did manage to escape to a go-kart track, where Heath was able to show his old skills behind the wheel, but soon they were heading back to Sydney for the Australian première of *A Knight's Tale*, when he reflected, 'I'm only in Australia every eight months or so, if I am lucky, so the whole fame thing has been very gradual. I haven't had time to be around all this madness, which is wonderful, great, but it's like being up in the roller-coaster and knowing it's going to come down.'

Yet again his anxieties about being 'sold' as consumer goods surfaced when he discussed the film and the inevitable publicity he had to do to coincide with its release: 'I had a real blast doing it and I am very proud of the film, and it's part of my job to promote it, but it makes me feel like a product. You know, I feel like a whore. It's like I'm promoting this product for, like, this Coca-Cola company.'

When he appeared at a press conference it was inevitable he would be asked about the state of his relationship with Heather. His reply was predictably – and understandably – tight-lipped: 'That's for me to know... and you never to know.' Another journalist then asked for his tips on love and received the reply, 'Oh f**k, I don't know!'

He did, however, respond in greater detail to more realistic questioning, saying that he was treating Hollywood as a 'big playground' and that he would love to return to Australia – for the right script: 'My base is LA, but I still call Australia home. I'm certainly comfortable in Hollywood but I would rather work here.' Of his sex-symbol status he simply stated, 'I don't sit around thinking about it. I guess there's a particular type who would, but I don't' and he repeated his mantra on the effects of fame, which he felt hadn't changed him: 'It just changes everyone else.'

He was more forthcoming in one interview he gave in California, where he admitted that he was suffering from a tequila-induced hangover after going out on the town with Rufus Sewell and Mark Addy and that he was more than capable of coping with the pressure of 'carrying' multi-million dollar films. 'Ultimately, it's someone else's $50-million, so I don't have the pressure of losing it. Basically,

I'm just showing up and acting. And my job on *A Knight's Tale* doesn't really differ from a $3.5-million movie. There is no amount of money that can change what I do between them saying "Action!" and "Cut!" Plus, *A Knight's Tale* has a fantastic ensemble cast so I never felt like the movie was riding on my shoulders. I don't think it's worth the time and the effort getting concerned about it. If it happens, it happens – it's not in my control. As far as I'm concerned, my career is just about me taking each day and dealing with it as it comes.'

But he admitted to one friend: 'I'm just beat. There isn't a bit of creative energy or spirit left in me; I really just need time to chill out and rest. Right now, the last thing I'm thinking of is the next job. We don't live to work, we work to live, you know but people forget that in Hollywood – I want to hold on to it.'

If his trip home hadn't been as ideal as he'd hoped, Heath decided to reverse the process by bringing 16 of his old school pals and other buddies from Perth to the Los Angeles première of *A Knight's Tale* at the 70-year-old Mann Village Theater. At Columbia's parking lot party, not far from the cinema, he sat and drank beers at a long table with the crew while Heather, in a flaming red dress and with large gold earrings, perched on his lap. 'Fame has not reached a point yet where I can't go out and enjoy myself with my mates,' he observed.

Close as Heath and Heather appeared that night – 'she's a beautiful girl. I'm very comfortable with her,' he admitted – a few weeks later he was spotted at the über-trendy Lotus bar in New York's meatpacking district entwined with an attractive companion until 5a.m. A fellow night-clubber said, 'They were all over each other.' The reason for Heath being out and about with another woman was simple: he and Heather had split after eight heady months together.

In early June her publicist confirmed: 'They are still good friends but they have broken up.' The great romance was over and Heath was already moving on.

CHAPTER 7

FILM FIGHTS –
FOR REAL

The casting of the lead roles in films can be a labyrinthine process at times. Moviegoers forever associate a particular actor with a role that he or she has made famous and it seems almost inconceivable that anyone else could have ever been considered for the part. Legend has it that Ronald Reagan might have won the Humphrey Bogart role in *Casablanca* and that James Coburn was first choice for the Spaghetti Westerns destined to make Clint Eastwood an international star. It was this type of lottery that resulted in Heath's role in his next film, the tense prison drama *Monster's Ball*.

The first choice for the part of Billy Bob Thornton's son was Heath's co-star from *The Four Feathers*, Wes Bentley, but when that didn't come to fruition, Heath stepped in at short notice to take on the role of suicidal Louisiana prison warder Sonny Grotowski.

The title of the film derived from centuries earlier when condemned men were known as 'monsters' and the night before their execution a party – a 'ball' – would be held by their jailers to give them a final, gruesome send-off.

Heath's character is a third-generation prison warder; grandfather Buck (Peter Boyle) is a racist, while dad Hank (Thornton) seems to hate the entire world including his family. A pivotal scene involves Sonny and Hank escorting prisoner Lawrence Musgrove (Sean 'P. Diddy' Combs) to the execution chamber and the younger guard – on his first such duty – cannot cope and is physically sick, much to his father's disgust. During his years of imprisonment the doomed man has been constantly visited by his wife Leticia (Halle Berry) and after his death she forms a relationship with Thornton's character, initially unaware of the role he played in her husband's death. Berry's love scenes with Thornton were regarded as some of the most frank and daring ever seen in a mainstream Hollywood picture.

Even the actress herself said of the encounter – a minute of which had to be cut from the final version as it was too explicit: 'I would like to believe that the world has gotten sophisticated to the point that it won't matter but it might become an issue. There will be those who want to kick up some dust over it, and I'm prepared for that. I would hope that people see the love scene in the context of the story. Well, that's what I hope.'

The film was laden with gloom in that several of its key characters ended up dead, but it will probably be best remembered not just, it must be said, for Heath's excellent performance but for the fact that it eventually enabled Halle Berry to become the first African-American woman to pick up an Oscar. Her highly emotional acceptance speech, with its seemingly never-ending list of tributes to anyone and everyone who helped her or who she admired, quickly became part of showbiz legend. It was fitting that she felt so overcome with her award because it was remarkable that the film – made for the remarkably low sum of $2.5 million – was ever made at all.

The script, by Milo Addica and Will Rokos, had been circulating Hollywood for years and names such as Robert De Niro, Tommy Lee Jones and even Marlon Brando had been linked with it at some time. Sean Penn and Oliver Stone were among those pencilled in to direct before it eventually reached Swiss-born Marc Foster. He was at pains to emphasise this wasn't simply another film on the evils of capital punishment, unlike the 1995 prison drama *Dead Man Walking*, directed by Tim Robbins: 'The film touches on more subject matters. *Dead Man Walking*, as good as it was, touched on a very specific issue and it was clear it was about capital punishment. This movie isn't really about capital punishment; it's about a lot of things – it's about the consequences of people's actions.'

The movie took five weeks to shoot and some scenes were filmed in the actual death chamber at the Louisiana State Prison in Angola. 'The creepiest thing was, we had so many people in the death chamber that they were making death chamber jokes,' Addica recalled. 'I looked at the chair, and there were initials carved into the chair.'

Actors by training, Addica and Rokos auditioned for, and landed roles, in their own movie: Rokos playing the warden and Addica a member of the death team. Addica said he would never forget the scene involving Heath and Thornton, where the older man attacks and punches his son because he has broken down prior to the execution: 'When Billy Bob confronts Heath in the prison bathroom, he says, "You messed up that last man's walk!" Then they have this physical fight and we run in there and break up the fight. We had to do that scene six or seven times. It got to the point I didn't want to go in and break the fight up because I was physically getting hurt.' Billy Bob Thornton recalled, 'When we were filming, the "warden" almost had to step in because he thought it was real. Heath's a tough kid.'

Addica subsequently told the *Los Angeles Times* that their screenplay was completed in early 1995 and the writers first thought of taking the project to Atlas Entertainment, the production company probably best known for the George Clooney Gulf War adventure, *Three Kings*. 'They were good guys, but it just didn't work out,' he recalled. 'After that, we made a deal at Fine Line Features but they had their own idea about what the movie should be. They put us through a development process we weren't happy with but they sent us to Sean Penn. He wanted to do it; he called De Niro.'

However, the addition of Penn and De Niro would have vastly increased production costs on the project and the rights to the film eventually reached Lee Daniels, Wes

Bentley's manager. 'It came to me for Wes with Sean Penn directing,' Daniels said. 'Marlon Brando and Robert De Niro and Wes would play the lead characters. We loved it and wanted to do it. I told the agent, "Let's do it."'

Another year passed, and Oliver Stone and Tommy Lee Jones were interested but that came to nought. Eventually the project was underway – boosted by having Oscar-winning Billy Bob Thornton on board – and once Wes Bentley dropped out, the script was sent to Heath. Although the majority of the publicity gathered before and after release centred on Halle Berry, *Monster's Ball* enabled Heath to become buddies with Sean Combs, alias Puff Daddy or P. Diddy, during the making of the film.

'I became pretty good friends with him. He was in an unusual position,' he said. 'This guy made $200 million last year from his rap clothing line alone and he is an incredibly powerful man. But he was in this really vulnerable position. He's never really done any acting before and he kind of had this baby face saying, "What do I do? Can anyone help me?" But he did a really good job.' Heath also resolved the potentially difficult position of how to address the would-be actor: 'He just told me to call him Sean.'

The movie was to be another fruitful addition to his body of work and one that would be welcomed as just around the corner lay another film that was to be a rare, if not unique, blot on his career.

The Four Feathers had not been a hit with either reviewers or the public, although Heath's performance had been well received. *A Knight's Tale* was both a commercial and critical success, however, marred by one matter over which Heath had no control. The publicity for the film referred to him as 'this year's hottest new star' and attributed the remark to one admiring film critic, a certain David Manning on a small-town newspaper in America. Mr. Manning had been fulsome in his praise of this, and several other films recently made by Columbia. His remarks turned out literally not to be worth the paper they were written on, though, when an enterprising journalist from *Newsweek* magazine discovered he didn't exist. Two employees of the publicity arm of the studio were subsequently suspended over the misrepresentation and cinemagoers offered some money back if they had paid to see *A Knight's Tale* and a small group of other films also favourably 'reviewed' by the non-existent Mr. Manning.

Brian Helgeland admitted: 'Yeah, we were one of the four movies at Sony [Columbia's parent company] that they blessed with a made-up review. On a movie that had dozens of good reviews, it was so arrogant. And then when that comes up, it sounds like the movie stinks and they have to make up reviews for it.'

Nevertheless, the omens were good when Heath reunited with director Helgeland. Not only that, but leading lady Shannyn Sossamon and *Full Monty* star Mark Addy were also on board for the thriller *The Sin Eaters*, later to be re-named *The Order*. 'I think Fox [the film's maker] was always kind of confused because as I went through casting I kept bringing in more and more people from *A Knight's*

Tale. We had a blast working together and I wanted to capture that. I even wanted to start with the villain from *Knight's Tale* [Rufus Sewell] and they kind of drew the line there. They were like, "No, no, we have to have someone from another place." They were like, "Enough is enough already," because even the little boy who plays Heath in the flashbacks in *A Knight's Tale*, he's in *The Order* also. That was like the last straw, I think,' Helgeland recalled.

The linking up again of the Prague-based ensemble seemed to bode well for the film with its theme of religious magic. The term 'sin-eater' referred to a person who, through ritual, would take on by means of food and drink the sins of a dead or dying person, thus absolving his or her soul and allowing them to rest in peace. Tradition has it that sometimes this is performed by a beggar – some small communities kept their own sin-eaters who could be brought to the bedside of a mortally ill person, who would then eat some bread that had been passed across the body of the dying one.

This ancient story was updated by Helgeland with Heath as Alex Bernier, a member of an order of priests known as Carolingians. When the head of the order dies, he is sent to Rome to investigate mysterious circumstances surrounding the death. The body bears strange marks on the chest, which may or may not be the sign of a sin-eater, William Eden (played by German actor Benno Furmann), a renegade who offers absolution, last rites and therefore a path to heaven outside the jurisdiction of the Church. Alex enlists the aid of his old friend Father Thomas (Addy) and of an artist (Sossamon), on whom he once performed an exorcism. Pretty quickly he finds himself at the centre of a supernatural thriller.

Although the premise and the cast of the film should have been an indicator of good things to come – this might well have been a movie to follow in the footsteps of *The Exorcist* or *Rosemary's Baby* – by January 2003 the trade paper *Variety* was sounding early warnings about its reception. The supposedly chilling effects used on occasion, far from frightening the audience at early screenings, were causing some of them to laugh. The 'food of sin' that was being drawn from bodies was, said the paper, being compared by some to 'flying calamari' and its release was put back. Not only that but at such a late stage it was given its new name, *The Order*.

With the release postponed until late summer and no showing for the critics. Helgeland was philosophical about the change of title: 'They didn't like *Sin Eater*. I accept that basically because they're saddled with having to sell it in a 15-second TV spot. When it's called *Sin Eater* and the spot is completely chewed up by just trying to explain what that is and they say that's a legitimate problem they're having, I can't ignore it.'

At least he didn't feel the film was being 'dumped' on the market: 'No, I don't think so, because they're spending a lot of money – I mean, relative to the budget, they're spending money to open it and they've got all the advertising out there. But it's like wherever you go, they have the Fox logo as small as possible. It's still getting released and everything; we'll see what happens. I have a strange feeling – and I'm usually very pessimistic – but I have a strange feeling that it's all going to work out.'

His hopes appeared to have been unfulfilled as when the film finally opened it was savaged by the critics. One said: 'Heath Ledger does his acting best, but nothing could save *The Order*. Forgive him, audience, for he hath sinned. Let us hope that *The Order* marks the nadir of Brian Helgeland's career, a fall from grace never to be repeated.

'Sadly, the talented, egg-headed writer of the Oscar-winning *L.A. Confidential* and writer/director of the style-spanning medieval romp *A Knight's Tale* has tarnished his reputation with *The Order*. The religious thriller is an unholy disorder comprised of a convoluted, didactic, almost comically anticlimactic plot, cinematography by Nicola Pecorini that seems inspired by (and is often as impenetrable as) Stygian darkness and a visual dynamic that, with the help of unnecessary effects, exaggerates the Church's routine juxtaposition of what is holy with what is horrific.

'The only redeeming features are the performances by two Helgeland faves: Heath Ledger as the Hamlet-like, Carolingian priest Alex Bernier and Mark Addy as his jovial fellow friar Thomas, two fine actors who cannot quite bring salvation to this abomination. A third Helgeland regular, Shannyn Sossamon, who was "discovered" for *A Knight's Tale*, gives another thin performance that calls into question the director's loyalty to her acting talents.'

But there was more… 'Snarling dogs, flocks of birds, a cross-dresser and hanging corpses appear suddenly out of the darkness. The soundtrack is alive with whispery spirits. There is a flashback to the construction of the Sistine Chapel, and even attempts at comedy… What does it all mean? Nine thousand Hail Marys and a celluloid act of contrition for a gifted filmmaker who needed a revised draft and more heavenly light.'

The *New York Post* labelled it, 'a moronic thriller' and continued, 'The best thing about *The Order* is its wintry Rome setting. The screenplay is packed with so many hilariously bad lines (it's hard to believe that writer-director Helgeland won an Oscar for co-writing *L.A. Confidential*) that the movie would be perfect material for a resurrected version of the TV spoof *Mystery Science Theater*. Sossamon, a mistress of wooden delivery, makes laughably unbelievable every scene she's in, except the inevitable sex sequence with Ledger.'

The *Boston Globe* was among the army of others keen to criticise and for once Heath didn't escape either: 'Another dreary horror film,' it described it. 'A stupendous bore about a priest going toe-to-toe with a Catholic sin-eater who cleanses the dying of their dirty deeds. Twenty-five years ago, the film would have starred George C. Scott as the kind of priest you could count on to devour the generic scenery and overcooked screenwriting with a knife and fork, his voice hoarse from all the acting. *The Order* just gives us the somnambulant stylings of Australia's Heath Ledger, who appears to have wandered in from a

Strokes concert. He's believable neither as a priest nor as an actor. But he's quite convincing as someone who likes his wispy facial hair and enjoys being paid to memorise Latin and Aramaic.'

The paper continued with a list of what it felt were the film's faults: '...there's director Brian Helgeland's brick of a script, which, if thrown hard enough, would kill anybody, too. Take the scene where Mara (Shannyn Sossamon), Alex's monotone ex- love, suddenly returns to his empty parish, having escaped from the loony bin just in time to accompany him to Rome. His first words to her are romantic: "When did they release you?" Hers, as you might infer, are psychotic. "I want to paint sunflowers," she drones, "but I didn't have the guts. Do you think I'm crazy?" Given what happened at their last meeting (at an exorcism Alex was performing), this reunion makes him leery. "You won't try to kill me this time?" he asks. "Cross my heart and hope to die," she replies. Great, now that that's settled: Baby, let's go slay some demons! If only this movie were that sort of sexy, stupid fun... Helgeland must have tricked Ledger, Sossamon, and Mark Addy who plays a fellow priest into making *The Order* back in 2001 while they were sipping mead on the set of *First Knight*. If you can believe it, Helgeland is the same guy who adapted *L.A. Confidential*.'

The *New York Daily News* was hardly any kinder: 'Uh-oh, there's meaningless whispering, muttering and wailing,' their reviewer wrote. 'It must be *The Order*, a supernaturally silly drama about priests, exorcism, sin-eaters and Heath Ledger struggling with such pious problems as how to keep his fake Euro accent in place. Twentieth Century Fox didn't screen this movie for critics, a sure sign that vile sins have been committed. Sure enough, Ledger as Alex Bernier is a big loser in this low-energy crypto-thriller.'

Perhaps the critics' views are best encapsulated by the *Chicago Sun Times*, who carried the headline: 'Don't go see this ghastly film, that's an Order.' The reviewer then continued: '...I have nothing good to say about *The Order*. I probably should have run screaming when the film's distributor, 20th Century Fox, refused to hold press screenings – movie studio speak for, "Our movie reeks, and we don't want anyone to know it." But, brave soul that I am, I pushed on, and found a way to see the movie. Big mistake. Writer-director Brian Helgeland's religious "thriller" is a mess. It's purportedly about a priest's crisis of faith after his mentor's death – the fallout of a young life shaken by unexplained death. But in Helgeland's hands, *The Order* is little more than a series of random plot points and religious babble mixed together and spat onto the screen in no particular order. We have characters falling in love without explanation or chemistry; we have people popping up in "sinister" plots that seem irrelevant to the story, as we know it. The worst part of all, though, is that none of these things matter. Because, frankly, we don't care.'

The final word should perhaps go to the *Los Angeles Times*, who said: '*The Order* slipped into US cinemas last

Friday and "is likely to appear at your local video store" any second now.'

If the reception for the film was a disappointment, Heath had been busy in the interim after filming wrapped in 2002. For such an eminently eligible young man it was hardly surprising that he wasn't without woman by his side for long. In the late 1990s before he became famous he met and dated beautiful blonde Melbourne model Christina Cauchi. The 5' 10" model first become known to a wider public in 1999 when she appeared on the cover of *Australian Style* magazine with her twin sister Helen, also a model, ruffling the hair of the then Victoria state Premier Jeff Kennett in a photo-shoot. His popularity ratings rose immediately.

Heath had even let slip her name in a question-and-answer session with *Cosmopolitan* in mid-Summer 2000, when asked: 'Do you have a girlfriend?' He answered, 'Yeah, she's a model named Christina Cauchi – we live together.' Asked, 'Are you the romantic type?' he replied, 'Well, I'm very fortunate with Christina because she and I will do nothing and it's quite romantic – just spending time together, being together. I love when we're sitting around, just the two of us, listening to music, with the lights off and lots and lots of candles, and we're holding hands.'

The couple were photographed together in Rome in 2000 before splitting up, but then got back together in late 2001 when they attended the Melbourne Cup in November that year although their only other public appearance was at the première of the Australian film *The Hard Word* in

May 2002. In total they dated for about eight months 'second time around' before Heath's sister Kate, who handled publicity inquiries about her brother during his stays in Australia, announced in July of that year that the couple had split. 'They both just wanted to clear that up,' Kate said. Asked if Heath was therefore single, her response was, 'Basically, yes.'

Heath had spent a lot of time in Australia that year and had reportedly bought an apartment in Melbourne during 2002 when he was in the country filming. And it wasn't just a film about any ordinary Australian; in fact it was arguably the most famous Aussie of all time, the bandit Ned Kelly. This was to open up yet a new phase in his career – and bring another beautiful actress into his life.

CHAPTER 8

'I PREFER OLDER WOMEN'

There is little doubt Ned Kelly is the most famous figure in Australian folk history. He was born in June 1855 and died in November 1880 – and in the intervening twenty-five and a half years he carved for himself a place in the country's history as strong and controversial today as it has ever been. Kelly occupies a place in the country's psyche similar to Robin Hood in England or Jesse James in America. To some Edward 'Ned' Kelly was a misunderstood political revolutionary, others regarded him merely as a mindless thief, murderer and gang-leader.

He was the first-born of an Irish Catholic couple. His father was an ex-convict – transported for the theft of two pigs – and his teenage mother a migrant. His father died while serving an Australian jail sentence and as the young breadwinner in the family Kelly left school in 1866 and began a string of criminal activities, including assault, theft, and horse-stealing, for which he was sentenced to three years' imprisonment. He spent some time as a timber worker upon his 1874 release before joining his stepfather in horse-stealing two years later. His brother Dan was sentenced to three months for damaging property and stealing horses. While attempting to arrest him, police were allegedly shot at by Kelly.

His family was sentenced for aiding and abetting – and £100 rewards were offered for Dan and Ned in 1878. In that year Joe Byrne and Steve Hart joined him to form the infamous Kelly Gang. In October of the same year, police attempting to capture them were surprised and an officer killed by the gang. The attempt to recapture Ned was soon followed by two further police deaths and the price on the brothers' heads was raised to £500, dead or alive.

Two daring armed robberies followed in December and February 1879 and the ever-increasing bounty was raised to £2,000. On Saturday, 27 June 1880, the Kelly Gang met at Glenrowan, a 'nowhere' town 115 miles north of Melbourne and the subsequent shoot-out provided an iconoclastic image of the man; protected by roughly-hewn iron helmet and body-shield and firing at the police who confronted him. He was outside in the bush while the rest of the gang held civilians hostage in the town's hotel and Kelly was finally brought down when the police realised he could be felled by shooting at his unprotected legs. Although there were rumours that his brother Dan and another gang member escaped, it is generally accepted Ned was the sole survivor. Kelly was sentenced to death in

October of that year and he was hung in Melbourne Jail on 11 November.

The confusion and the merging of fact and fiction overshadowing his life remained with him until the end. One famous version of his final words was, 'Such is life,' while another was the line, 'Ah, well, I suppose it has come to this.' A third has it that he simply uttered an audible sigh. Already a cult figure to many Australians, a large number at that time would have descended from convicts themselves; on his death he became an anti-hero and a figure to be admired by some for what they saw as his opposition to authority. On the back of this he became a quintessential figure in the short history of Australia – and the world's first 'film star'.

Immediately after his death his name was immortalised. Books and stories were written about him, plays performed and there were countless songs and then the exciting infant medium of film. The Australian-made *The Story of the Kelly Gang* (1906) is now recognised as the world's first feature-length film and had a then-unprecedented running time of 70 minutes. For a brief period in those Edwardian days the Australian film industry actually made more feature-length films than either America or Britain. Then came *The Kelly Gang* (1920), *When the Kellys Were Out* (1923) and *When the Kellys Rode* (1934). Those early films were enlivened by sound effects such as blank shots being fired off-stage, pebbles shaken to imitate the sound of rainfall and even coconuts banged together to reproduce the sound of galloping horses! It might sound comical now, but the earliest film of the gang was actually banned in Victoria when it was released on the grounds that it glorified bushrangers – outlaws in the bush such as Ned Kelly and his gang – and might provoke rioting. The ban lingered on for decades, even though the bushranger movies were quickly overtaken in popularity by Westerns with 'Cowboys and Indians' themes.

Nevertheless *The Glenrowan Affair* came out in 1951 and then there was *Stringybark Massacre* (1967), which was based on Kelly's life. Soon afterwards came *Ned Kelly*, starring Rolling Stone Mick Jagger in the title role, complete with a much-derided Irish accent; during its making this led to a protest by the Australian Actors Union over the casting of the English rock star. There were even complaints from descendants of Kelly's family and others over the film being shot in New South Wales rather than the Victoria locations where most of the events actually took place. In 1980 there was a highly praised mini-series called *The Last Outlaw* and even a 1993 satire, *Reckless Kelly*.

So Heath had not just inherited a historical legacy but a cinematic one too. And this was to prove to be more than just a film: it was to have an effect on his personal life too. A fairly routine item in an Australian newspaper in April 2002 listing other actors in the movie read, in part, like this: 'The film, which will star Heath Ledger in the title role, will also feature appearances by Australian actors Rachel Griffiths, Joel Edgerton, Peter Phelps and Russell Dykstra, as well as British actor Orlando Bloom. The latter will play bushranger Joe Byrne; Griffiths will play a woman called Mrs Scott (who is seduced by Byrne); Edgerton and Dykstra are set to appear as Kelly cohorts Aaron Sherritt and Isiah Wild Wright; and Peter Phelps will play policeman Thomas Lonigan.' Tellingly, and very importantly for Heath, there was also a line stating: 'An announcement on the female lead will be made next week.'

Filming began in the summer of 2002, not in Glenrowan, by now too modern and also too far from Melbourne, but on location just an hour or so north of the city. Heath knew he had some very large and illustrious shoes to fill if he was to successfully cope with both the expectations and the legacy that the name brought to the film. He had one unashamed supporter alongside him throughout, however, the man who thought him ideal for the part: director Gregor Jordan who had been in charge of the influential *Two Hands* in Australia just a few years earlier. His budget had increased in the intervening years and the new film was reported to be costing around £15 million, although Heath was receiving just £30,000 compared to the £2 million he pocketed for *A Knight's Tale*.

'I was given the script by executive producer Tim White and I was interested in it as a concept,' Jordan said. 'But I said to Tim, the only way to make this movie is with Heath. To me he was the only person who could play the role. So I rang Heath and told him about it, he read the script and said, "OK, let's do it." And so it was only really when Heath said, "yes," that I said "yes." You need someone who is the right age, physically tall, strong and charismatic. I also wanted him to be Australian. So when you put that list together, there is really only one person to play the role. People have been coming up to me at parties, saying, "It's so fantastic that you're making this film", and then they fix you with a stern gaze and say, "Don't f**k it up."

'Number one: Heath's the right age. Ned was 25 when he died; Ned was also a very charismatic guy. When he walked into a room, he'd command attention without even trying. Heath is the kind of guy who just has that thing, too. He has lots of charisma. If you want to make a film of this size, you've got to have a star on board. He fits the bill and, as an incredible bonus, he's Australian. For a young actor, what is there? There's Hamlet, but for an Australian, Kelly is the ultimate role. Heath's the right age for the role, has the level of charisma and the star power to justify the budget, and also he's an Australian. That combination is unique. For leading men under the age of 25 there's Leonardo DiCaprio, whose salary is stratospheric, and then basically there's just Heath Ledger and Josh Hartnett.'

Executive producer Tim Bevan said Heath's presence would overcome the average American's ignorance concerning Kelly: 'The UK, New Zealand and Australia are fine. Everybody knows who Ned Kelly was. But you need to put elements into the movie that are going to make it attractive to a broader audience. We were lucky to get Heath and to fill that cast out so that it's sexy and inviting. The equivalent in Britain when we're doing a romantic comedy is, if you get Hugh Grant try to get Emma

Thompson and Kate Winslet as well. Then these films begin to feel bigger than they actually are, which is the trick in getting them away outside their indigenous audience.'

Heath was equally enthusiastic, and that keenness helped to explain why he was prepared to make the film for less than his going rate: 'I think my agents are beginning to hate me,' he could laughingly say. 'They have all these ideas and ambitions for me, and I don't want any of it. I've done nothing special and suddenly I'm up there being pimped and whored as part of a marketing campaign. Really, it's like being in a Toyota factory; you're just another door being thrown on a car.

'Ned was an incredible part and a story I feel very passionately about. I'm Australian, so clearly it is a dream role. It was the best opportunity I have had to sink my teeth into a part. I've looked up to him since I was a kid. I remember thinking that I'd love to play him. He represents a lot to me, such as dignity and sticking by your family and mates. I'm totally on Ned's side because what the cops did to him was terrible and he had just cause to stand up against them. But the film isn't something my agents would have wanted me to do. When I was in *10 Things I Hate About You* they wanted me to do one teen movie after another. Then I was in *A Knight's Tale* and they thought, "Great, let's get him into blockbusters." They haven't realised that I do this because I love it, not for the money. I don't need to buy 100 homes and 50 cars; I plan to have a long career, I want to be on your film screen for a while to come.

'Gregor is a really good friend of mine – I had worked with him before and I knew it was going to be fun. And I knew Gregor was the guy for the job because he had a very clear picture on what he wanted; he always does. I read a lot about Ned Kelly as a kid and fantasised about what it would be like back then for him. In a way I have looked up to him quite a bit throughout my life, so it has been quite eerie stepping into his shoes at this point.'

Heath read Ned Kelly's 'Jerilderie Letter' – a document over 50 pages long outlining the outlaw's grievances and calling for justice – numerous times and he remained stunned by, 'just how passionate he was in there, and so definite, so precise, and how sure he was about his cause. It was very exciting to give life to these words, to give life to this legend and have a guess at what he was like. I just didn't allow myself to feel that much pressure. I didn't want my performance to be polluted by these pressures of getting it right and making it true and real. I had an idea in my head, I read up on him and I looked into his eyes. There is a portrait of him two days before he was hanged – it's all in his eyes: he is very dignified, he is very proud, and that was enough. I just trusted my own instinct and went for it. I'll certainly take a piece of Ned with me; he's certainly going to be carried around in my heart and my mind for a long time. It's given me the courage to stand up and be true to what I believe in.'

One of the important matters that had to be sorted out before filming started was exactly what Heath would look like during the film. The few images of Kelly's face from that Victorian period showed a young man almost hiding behind a strange, long beard. To be historically accurate, that was the look Heath should have, but for a handsome young leading man to be hidden behind such a luxuriant growth might not be too clever at the box-office. Studio chiefs were worried that their very-bankable stars, Heath and Orlando Bloom, might have those good looks of theirs undercover. 'They didn't want us to wear beards at all,' Heath was to say, although the film's spokeswoman Emma Cooper stressed that the beard-or-no-beard argument did not affect filming. 'Heath began make-up tests in November with [make-up artist] Jenny Shircore to decide upon Ned's look,' she said. 'Heath actually has three looks in the film: he starts as a young Ned with no beard and works up to a full beard when Ned becomes the bushranger.' She added that there had been talks about beard-length between the studio, Ledger and Jordan, and the actor had been most insistent on historical accuracy: 'Heath was very adamant he wanted the full beard look to play Ned Kelly and Gregor was supportive of this. It definitely was sorted out before we started shooting and the three looks were agreed on by everyone (including the studio). There is no way we could have started filming without this being finalised.'

Filming had indeed been underway for some weeks when that 'female' lead flew in for her brief appearance in the movie. Naomi Watts was only scheduled to be working on the film for six days, but it was to be a role that changed her life – and Heath's. She had just been voted one of the

50 most beautiful people in the world and was, in Hollywood parlance, 'hot'. Her roles in *Mulholland Drive* and the recent movie, *The Ring*, had brought her to an international audience.

The actress, born in England but raised in Australia – and like Heath a former member of the *Home and Away* cast – had a busy schedule and had just finished filming 3 movies in quick succession. Her *Ned Kelly* role as Julia Cook, a squatter's wife, was one of the fictitious characters written into the script that director Jordan openly said mingled fact and fiction. In Watts' case the character was one from a dream sequence featured in the book *Our Sunshine* by Robert Drewe, on which the film was based.

She admitted later, 'I was almost thinking of ways I could get out of it because I thought it would be physically and humanly impossible, but once I got here I thought, "OK, this is the right thing to do – I'm glad I came."' The Australian weather might have been cold and windy for those few days in June while she was filming on location, but it did nothing to dampen the attraction the two actors felt for each other. Heath had been dating Christina Cauchi as recently as the end of May, but their on-off relationship was 'off' again by the time Naomi arrived on the set. She hadn't met Heath – 10 years her junior – before filming but she was fulsome in her praise for him. 'Working with Heath Ledger, who's an incredibly talented actor, and Rachel Griffiths and Geoffrey Rush, were major draw points for me,' she said.

During a scene with her on-screen husband she and

Heath, both in character, are called on to exchange furtive glances. In her next scene she watches her children playing in the garden as Kelly rides up the drive and she then admonishes the outlaw for risking being caught.

Later, she was to recall the instant she knew Heath was the man for her: 'It was a scene when he jumped on his horse and said goodbye to me. I suddenly felt like I was in *Wuthering Heights*. It was a beautiful, old-fashioned moment.' Showing that life goes on as normal even on a film set, two portable televisions had been brought onto the set so the crew and actors not directly involved in filming could watch an England v Brazil match in the World Cup finals. Watts was keenly supporting the English and moved quickly between the set and the televisions to keep abreast of the game. Eventually she and Heath – having changed out of costume – sat down on the floor alongside each other, watching the game with the rest of the crew.

Soon after the match finished, everyone made the short journey south to Melbourne and that weekend Heath and Naomi were photographed at a city nightclub sitting either side of Rachel Griffiths. On the Monday morning the pair played out their love scene on camera on the closed set. It had been a dramatic introduction, both on and off-screen, and it seems inevitable to conclude that there was a great deal more to Watts' comments about her leading man on the *Ned Kelly* film website than met the eye when she subsequently said: 'There are movie stars and then there are actors and Heath to me is both. To be a movie star, you

have to be good-looking or have a great voice that
resonates, that connects with people, or you have to have
something behind the eyes: an intelligence, a sadness, a
warmth. Heath's got them all and therefore he is a movie
star and an actor. His commitment to being there for other
people was pretty mind-blowing. On the first day I noticed
that and I was like, "Wow, this is impressive." I was just
really excited about working with him.' She certainly was,
although remarkably it was months before their
relationship became public knowledge. At the end of
August the *Sun-Herald* in Australia reported breathlessly:

Two of Australia's hottest young movie stars, Naomi
Watts and Heath Ledger, have fallen for each other on
the set of their latest film. Romance blossomed
between Ledger, 23, and Watts, 33, on the Victorian
set of *The Kelly Gang*, in which they play Ned Kelly
and his lover. Although they are keeping their
relationship low-key, the pair has been an item for
two months, Ledger's older sister and publicist Kate
Ledger confirmed. The couple tried to keep their
burgeoning real-life affair under wraps, never
showing affection in front of director Gregor Jordan
or their co-stars. However, once filming wrapped up,
the pair were spotted at a number of Sydney hot spots,
including Hugo's at Bondi Beach, where they were
seen canoodling at a corner table. Watts and Ledger
have returned to their adopted home of Los Angeles,
where she is about to start work opposite Sean Penn

and Benicio Del Toro in a film called *21 Grams* and he is scheduled to do publicity for his latest film, *The Four Feathers*.

Kate Ledger confirmed her brother's new status when she said: 'I don't have much to say but, yes, he is definitely seeing her. I've met Naomi and she's a gorgeous girl.'

The couple was soon spotted shopping for furniture in Sydney and rather bizarrely clashed with Sean Combs' bodyguards when they danced 'too close' to his table at the New York nightclub, the heavies not realising that he and Heath were friends from their filming days.

The cat was well and truly out of the bag and by the time the world première was approaching, in March 2003, Watts was referring to Heath as her 'boyfriend' and was happy to say they were sharing a house together in the Hollywood Hills. It appeared all domestic bliss, with Heath busy in the kitchen cooking up stir-fries for the couple. Their age difference was not a topic they dwelt on, she said, although she did worry about her own age: 'A woman's career is shorter than a man's and in your late 30s and early 40s the roles dry up and that's depressing. All I can do is push and break the rules and have the courage to take challenging roles.'

As the day of the *Ned Kelly* world première in Melbourne drew even closer, Australian newspapers were calling the couple the country's 'Royal Celebrity Couple'. They were spotted at the Bluebar in Melbourne one night and the next day seen looking for shoes in Zomp. 'They were looking very cuddly and very happy,' someone who saw them reported. 'Heath was wearing a green hooded top and was unshaven. Once word spread through the store that it was them, Heath started to look very uncomfortable.'

They were very publicly together again when they attended a fashion show with an anti-war theme by Heath's designer friend Shem Watson, so it was no surprise that they brought the centre of Melbourne to a halt when they arrived at the première at The Regent Theatre. There had been a pre-film party at Melbourne Jail, where Kelly had been hung, and the crowds were five-deep in the area around the cinema, waving placards and calling out the stars' names as the celebrities began arriving shortly before 7 p.m. Naomi wore a halter-neck, floral-print silk dress by Christian Dior while Heath was in a suit designed by Shem Watson.

Watts had had some high-profile Hollywood relation-ships: James Woods (twice her age), Kyle MacLaughlin (*Twin Peaks* co-star) and Ed Burns (long and involved) – and she had learned a few lessons: 'It's better to fall in love and risk the pain and heartbreak of having it end than not take risks… there's no love without fear. You just have to get through that fear and go for it.'

The reception the couple received was repeated when they attended the Perth première soon afterwards: Heath all cool in black and wearing sunglasses, Naomi looking every inch a film star in her cream Emanuel Ungaro dress. Surprisingly, Heath admitted that he was extremely nervous about seeing the film: 'All I've seen is a rough cut, so I'm looking forward to seeing it completed. My palms are dripping with sweat. We are all very proud of the movie and it is our opinion about Ned. There is no one "truth" about this guy, how he walked, how he talked, how he lived... This is just a stab in the dark, it's our interpretation.'

Once he had seen the final version he was in a fairly relaxed mood, however, when interviewed a few days later about his attitude to work, the film and life with Naomi: 'The time between action and cut is sacred to me. I really enjoy it,' he said. 'The actual turning up and sinking my teeth into that stuff I adore. The work side of it is talking about it a year later; it's all in your head. You can read a billion books about the guy, but it won't tell you squat about how he held himself or how he walked. It's about finding one little thing, whether it's a glint in the eye or just one piece of inspiration, and holding on to it and trusting it. There were so many different opinions on what this guy was like I just had to trust my own opinion and give it a shot and not care what people thought.

'I loved every second of playing that guy: I think he represents the independent spirit; he represents pride and dignity. He's like the classic Aussie. For the final shot of the movie the entire cast and crew were jam-packed behind the monitor watching it. It was just dead quiet, none of us wanted it to be over; none of us wanted Ned to die. Gregor and I were a little nervous. It was like, "Man, should we do this? Dude, if we mess this up we're going to be selling fish and chips in Byron Bay!" And that may not be a bad thing, but it was do or die. Then we thought, "Screw it, let's just do it!" I think most of the higher classes of Australia do appreciate this guy because that's where they came from. F**k them if they don't! You look at the portraits they paint of Ned and he always looks 50 years old, but they were f***ing young, man.'

He was even relaxed enough to tell one interviewer over the phone: 'I'm feeling great, mate: I'm in Australia, I've got my mates here, it's the best. I've been sitting on my butt in LA for the last eight months doing nothing – cooking, doing the washing... just living. And all the while there's been this buzz building back here and there's been posters everywhere and it's kinda surreal.'

He briefly let slip that at home in California Naomi made him do the washing-up, but he was a lot more forthcoming about her acting ability: 'I think she's brilliant. And I don't know if that's a biased view, but most people would agree she's probably the most talented actress out there.' He also tellingly made a rare comment on the age gap between them, as indeed there had been between himself and Heather Graham: 'I prefer to date older women because they try to act younger, unlike younger girls who try to act older. I know it's weird that I'm such a private person but still date high-profile women, but I can't let the celebrity thing influence my decisions on who I see; that would be unfair to myself.'

CHAPTER 9

NAOMI AND AN
ON-OFF LOVE

If Heath Ledger's rise to fame had been meteoric, the same could not be said of Naomi Watts. She had worked for years for her 'overnight success' and was even on the verge of quitting acting altogether a short time before her big break eventually happened.

Born on 29 September 1968 in Shoreham, Kent, her father Peter was a sound engineer and her mother was the actress Tyranny 'Miv' Watts. Her parents' voices were heard on Pink Floyd's classic album *Dark Side of the Moon*, her father being a road manager and sound engineer who worked with the band.

Naomi's parents separated when she was 3 and four years later her father died. Her mother, who she described as a 'hippy', then moved Watts and her elder brother Ben to their maternal grandparents' home on the island of Anglesey in north Wales. Because her grandmother was

Australian, this meant it was easier for Miv and her son and daughter to move Down Under, which she did when Naomi was in her early teens. Watts subsequently said: 'I consider myself British and have very happy memories of the UK. I spent the first 14 years of my life in England and never wanted to leave. When I was in Australia I went back to England a lot.'

She attended several acting schools in Sydney and it was there that she met and became friends with the biggest female star ever to come from Australia, Nicole Kidman: 'It was at this model call for some trashy swimsuit job. We had to wait for ages and we just started chatting. Neither of us got the job, but we shared a taxi home because we lived in the same area, and we've been friends from then on. We're still very close. We talk all the time and we tell each other everything,' she said.

The pair's friendship was to prove long lasting and they have comforted each other through the trials and tribulations of both their private and professional lives ever since. Indeed, for a while when Kidman was with Tom Cruise and being fêted for her beauty and her string of film performances, it seemed that Naomi might be doomed to become known merely as 'Nicole Kidman's close friend'.

In 1986 Naomi went to work in Japan as a model; she later called it one of the worst experiences of her life and when she returned to Australia, she was employed by a local department store and then as assistant fashion editor with an Australian fashion magazine. A part in a small play gave her the determination to try her hand at acting once more. As well as the obligatory spell in *Home and Away*, she appeared on television in *The Brides of Christ*, a series set in a Sydney convent school, in which she played one of the students, even though she was 23 at the time. The series was notable not only for the boost it gave her career but an appearance in one episode of a very young Russell Crowe. If this was meant to be the springboard for her success, it just didn't work though.

Years in Los Angeles failed to provide that vital step up, despite appearing in the 1995 cult film *Tank Girl*, and there seemed nowhere to go: 'My good friend Nicole Kidman kept telling me, "You're very talented. Please don't give up."' Defiantly she thought: 'I kept reminding myself that acting was the only thing that I really knew and that it was the only thing that I loved to do. I kept thinking, "You're good, you're good, you're good."' But the rejections started to get to her: 'When you are vulnerable you start to believe that stuff and let it become the truth. I let myself into a place where I shut down and I think I became un-hireable. I tried to walk away a number of times but something would grab me and hook me back. It was rejection after rejection and I took it on, which I think is a very human thing not to.'

Her big break was just around the corner, however. It came in the shape of *Mulholland Drive*, with controversial director David Lynch at the helm. She had already won her part in the production when it was all set to become a television series but when that fell through, she had to wait until it eventually made the big screen: 'The worst time was after I'd shot *Mulholland Drive* but no one had seen it. I wasn't working, I didn't have health insurance and one day I got this notice that I was being thrown out of my apartment because I was late on my rent for three months in a row. The Actors' Strike was pending and I didn't know what I was going to do. To say that times were tough is an understatement,' was how she summed up that dark period.

Those tough times were soon to end. The film premièred at the Cannes Film Festival, where it was highly praised, and it received similar accolades at festivals in both New York and Toronto. With its complicated psychological thriller plot, which left cinema-goers wondering what was a dream and what was reality in the two-hour film, it also attracted a large audience.

One thing was definitely for real: Naomi Watts had become a star.

That status was confirmed with the massively successful *The Ring*, a remake of a Japanese horror film in which anyone who sees a certain video is dead within seven days. Her co-star, incidentally, was Martin Henderson, Heath's old flatmate from Sydney, just a few years earlier. The film was released soon after filming on *Ned Kelly* was completed and by the time it premièred in October 2002 she and Heath were very much an item.

The couple strolled hand in hand at the Hollywood Film Festival gala, where Naomi received a breakthrough award. And after *The Ring* première, the two were spotted kissing passionately back at the Château Marmont, the 'hotel of the stars' in Hollywood.

Heath was, as always, unforthcoming when asked about his relationship with Naomi, replying: 'It's one thing to be romantic when it comes to love, but we need romance in our soul in a broader sense.' He was also to say, 'I still have so much to do it would be unfair to commit to marriage.'

Naomi too was still reluctant to talk about the relationship: 'I don't want to be rude or anything,' she told one questioner, 'it's just so new and it's our own delicate, beautiful thing and that's all I'm going to say. We're discovering what it is.' At least she was more forthcoming when she added, 'There was a time I was very much blaming the way I felt on LA, that it was a vacuum of creativity, of humour or anything organic, and I was really angry at the place. But then today I feel completely different – I love LA,' adding, 'You could say that my "overnight" has taken a long, long time.' No wonder she was now able to state, 'In the last year I haven't had to audition for anything and to me that's the meaning of success.'

It wasn't just the film world that the two had in common. In early 2003 they took part in a demonstration in Melbourne over the American attack on Iraq. Demonstrators chanted, 'George Bush, go to hell, we won't fight a war for Shell!' and brandished banners saying, 'No blood for oil' and 'We are all terrorists'. In a television interview, Heath vigorously defended his stance and admitted his very public opposition to the war might not be a good career move: 'Yeah, but at the end of the day what am I going to blow up, my career? And at the end of the day my career is so insignificant in this war, it just is, and I'm willing to lose a few jobs over it.'

He also supported Oscar-winning US documentary maker Michael Moore, who used his acceptance speech to say that the troops had been sent to Iraq for 'fictitious' reasons. Ledger clapped his hands and described Moore's speech as 'fantastic' after it was read to him – 'The unfortunate truth is none of us know enough and we will never know enough. This is the first time in the history of our country that we are an aggressor and we are not an aggressive nation or people.'

With the position they both occupied in Australian life, he and Naomi were understandably referred to as the country's 'Golden Couple' yet paradoxically this didn't open every door to them. During their stay in the country they were refused entry to nightclubs in both Melbourne and Sydney. 'We were refused entry to a nightclub in Melbourne on the weekend,' said Naomi. 'This guy was like, "You can't come in here," and we were like, "Why?"' In fact, it was Ledger's tracksuit pants that had offended the bouncer but once he realised the star's identity somehow the dress code didn't matter. 'It's a laugh in retrospect, but at the time it was a bit annoying,' she continued. 'We just wanted to have a boogie and a couple more drinks. I think the bouncer sussed who it was, and was like, "Oh, no, no, no, you can come in!" and we were like, "Goodbye, it's not worth it."' 'The same happened in Sydney,' said Heath. 'We were turned away because I was wearing a rugby shirt. Not only was

I not recognised, I wasn't even allowed into a bar that I'd been in before.'

Their lives were full to overflowing: film stardom, house-sharing in the groovy Los Feliz area of Los Angeles and political activism. They were busy too; Heath was back in Prague filming *The Brothers Grimm* with Terry Gillam and Naomi had been chosen for the starring female role in *King Kong*, a massive blockbuster that would cement her place in the upper echelons of stardom. The couple seemed to have everything in common – or did they?

At the end of September 2003 came the bombshell announcement that they had separated. Heath's sister Kate confirmed the split, blaming conflicting work commitments: 'Heath Ledger and Naomi Watts have made the decision to go their separate ways,' she said in her role as spokeswoman. She would not reveal when the couple had broken up but said it had been 'pretty recent' and added, 'At this time in their lives, both are busy building their careers which are taking them in different directions, but they remain close friends.'

There had been rumours that all was not well in their relationship, but the announcement of the separation contradicted a remark of Naomi's, reported almost at the same time as the split, when she said she was, 'dying to have a child. We'd both like to have kids at some point. But right now, we're both busy with our careers.' Fans had hardly become used to the parting of the ways when they opened up their morning newspapers to read that the two were an item once more!

They had only been apart for a few weeks before being drawn to each other again. This time Kate Ledger informed the world that although Heath was still filming in the Czech Republic they had reunited. The reconciliation became very public when they both came to Australia in early December for Kate's wedding in Perth to long-term partner Nathan Buckey. Naomi was due to promote her new film *21 Grams*, in which she played the lead female role opposite Hollywood heavyweight Sean Penn and Academy Award winner Benicio Del Toro. The film was to earn her universal praise and secure for her an Oscar nomination for Best Actress but before that promotional round began, she linked up with Heath for the pre-Christmas wedding in Western Australia.

So great was the interest in the two and their on-off-on love that details of the wedding were kept secret from the 160 guests to avoid turning it into a media circus. On the morning of the big day Heath and several male members of his family played golf at the privately owned Dunsborough Lakes Golf Club before the ceremony at the exclusive Empire Retreat, a health spa and boutique hotel near Yallingup, about three hours' drive from Perth.

Heath's grandfather John Ramshaw, who lived nearby, said the wedding was shrouded in secrecy: 'It is a very exciting day for all of us. The details are a big secret; we haven't been told where the ceremony is being held. All we know is that a big coach will come and pick us up and take us there.'

Naomi, who was rumoured to have been lined up to be

a bridesmaid before her brief separation from Heath, wore a mid-calf length floral dress with a handkerchief hem over gold stilettos. Her hair was pinned back in a ponytail. Heath was certainly dressed more smartly than his usual night-clubbing outfits in a black suit with a white shirt and dark sunglasses for the 5pm lakeside ceremony. It was understandable that, on his sister's big day, he wanted to ensure that the family had their privacy.

Yet a few days later he and Naomi were out together swimming at Bronte Beach, Sydney, and then later they talked with family and friends at East Circular Quay before the city première of *21 Grams*. Then they were spotted on a luxury boat pulling into the city's Woolloomooloo Wharf, clutching a bottle of champagne and two glasses, and heading for the exclusive Otto restaurant on the wharf – a favourite with, among others, former US President Bill Clinton, Sarah Michelle Gellar, Sir Michael Caine and Jerry Springer, where they enjoyed a candlelit dinner for two.

The couple who both knew Sydney well, of course, were even reported to have been looking for somewhere to buy in the eastern part of the city, in the £2 million price range. One of their priorities was that the home should not be overlooked – essential for two stars who valued their privacy. The desire to lead a life away from public attention was reaffirmed when interviewers were told that if they questioned Naomi about her relationship with Heath the question-and-answer session would be immediately terminated. Nevertheless she was in the public spotlight with her nomination for an Oscar being announced and she did let slip to one journalist, 'Well, I definitely want to know what it feels like to be a mum.'

There was nowhere for her to hide a few days after she and Heath had been to a David Bowie concert in Los Angeles when she was interviewed by one of the biggest names in American television, veteran Barbara Walters. During her long career Walters had quizzed Boris Yeltsin, Fidel Castro, Margaret Thatcher and Michael Jackson among others and her interview with President Clinton's girl-pal Monica Lewinsky attracted an astonishing 73 million viewers so she pulled no punches when she said to Naomi: 'You said you used to date men 10 years older, but Heath is 10 years younger, so what is having a younger man? Does it bring a different something?' 'Wait, wait? He's how old? And I'm how old?' Naomi said, endeavouring to joke her way out of a corner. 'I'm not so good with numbers, Barbara.'

'He's 10 years younger. Is that correct?' Walters was not one to be sidetracked easily and Naomi told her, 'That is correct.' Eventually the star had to admit, 'Love is love. You fall for the person, not an age. Not a number.'

Around the time of the Walters' interview Naomi was busy arranging her group for Oscar night; Heath and her mother and fashion photographer brother Ben were to accompany her. She'd broken news of her nomination to her mother in a call from the States in the middle of the Australian night saying, 'Mum, I know it's 4.30a.m. in the morning, but get your arse out of bed, I've got some really good news!'

'That's how I found out,' Miv said. 'Everyone was so completely over the moon about it. My best girlfriend rang me from London and screamed down the phone, "You're an Oscars' mum!" Nobody can believe it. It's a fantasy world, isn't it? It's things you never, ever imagined happening in your life and they've suddenly happened. It's just amazing for Naomi. It is enough for me that Naomi has been honoured by her profession through an Academy nomination. It's enough of a win and everything else is just the icing on the cake. She's a real Aussie girl. She knows that when something's not won easily and you have to go through pain to do it, you're a better human being at the other end.'

But, in the meantime, she was gearing up for her first Oscars Ceremony. 'Naomi's worked so hard for this,' she told the *Sun-Herald* in Australia. 'I've been there during the lows, moments of deep despair where she's had the worst possible time, when she's been going to auditions and people have been foul to her. I stayed with her during her lowest ebb, I think, when she was about ready to jack it in. And then along came our dearest David Lynch. We all have a lot to be thankful to him, for having the insight to see what a wonderful actress she is.'

It would have been a fairytale ending had Naomi won the Oscar for Best Actress, but with the vote going to Charlize Theron she was forced to console herself by sitting on Heath's knee at the after-Oscar *Vanity Fair* party. He had been loving and tactile throughout the evening, openly holding her hand and stroking her back, before and during the proceedings.

But the questions about their relationship – and that age gap – kept coming. Naomi told one interviewer, 'Heath is an old soul and he's someone I connected with. The age thing means nothing to me. I've dated people 10 years older, 10 years younger, doesn't make any difference either. I suppose I'm ready to nest. Everyone dreams of a little corner of the world they can call their own.' She also told American style magazine *W*, 'My mother is dying for me to have children and, quite frankly, I've been dying for it since I was 19, but I hadn't met the right man. It's interesting. At the age of 35, my career couldn't be going better but we all know that fertility slows down at this point, so it's about making choices. I really do want to experience a baby.'

Heath's take on that was, 'having a relationship is not challenging at all. I think people desperately try to make it challenging for us by assuming and creating stories or just being interested in us. But love is love. If you're in love, it's easy and it's hard in a good way. Our relationship is everything a healthy relationship should be.' He said that he was 'very happy,' but added in almost the same breath, 'No, I'm not getting married.' On Naomi's acting ability, he did admit, 'I only worked with her a little bit on *Ned Kelly*, but I've obviously lived with her when she was working on other projects and I've seen how committed she is. She knows how to harness her emotions and express them in a beautifully seductive and naive way.' As for her remark that 'I really do want to experience a baby', he said: 'I've always dreamed of having children. I don't see anything wrong with having them when you're young.'

But the spring of 2004 was to prove a troubled time for Heath, who was filming *Lords of Dogville* in Los Angeles at the time. *Ned Kelly* received mixed reviews from many American critics and Stateside audiences struggled with the film without the historical knowledge of the central character that audiences in Australia already had.

There was bad news on the personal side too.

The tabloid magazines sold by supermarket check-outs in America are as ferocious in their pursuit of celebrities as any publications in the world. Heath and Naomi were in their sights by this time and in April *Star* magazine reported they had separated again. According to the magazine, Naomi had allegedly told a 'friend' that the reason for the split was Heath's 'hard-partying ways', adding, 'He acted like he wanted the same things but was only saying what I wanted to hear. He doesn't want to get married and have kids. He's immature and unruly; he's always out clubbing with his friends. He's so immature it makes me look stupid for being with him.' Just to rub salt in the wound, the *Star* even said he'd been spotted at a club with another film actress, the dark-haired Winona Ryder.

Soon afterwards Naomi was careful not to name names when she was forced to talk about her private life while promoting her film *We Don't Live Here Anymore*, a tale of suburban wife-swapping but she did admit, 'I have been cheated on. You always fear it. It's horrible. I've never been married, but I've been forced to face infidelity and been hurt by it.

'I know what it's like to bottle emotions. I've definitely

been guilty of that at times, but I know if I keep my emotions in, I'll explode over the most ridiculous thing. Suddenly, it all comes bubbling out and I'll be completely irrational. I have married friends who have been through infidelity and gotten through it. I've had friends who've had the desire to be with someone else in an animal way and I think that's completely human.' And even if she had been cheated on, she said this didn't necessarily mean the end of a relationship: 'I love it when I hear someone say that they had that desire and got honest with their partner and talked about it – rather than the partner going, "Damn you!" and getting all jealous and reactive. In some cases, the partner has gone, "OK, that hurts, but I do understand it."'

It's fitting that she should have the final say on her love affair with Heath. In November 2004 she placed on record that the couple's age difference played no part in their relationship ending: 'I think it's about life experience and not about age. I fell in love with a soul and a person and his life experience was rich enough that it stimulated me. I have nothing but good things to say about my romance with Heath Ledger. We loved each other. I'm close with his family; he's close with mine. He is a friend and we'll always remain in contact.'

At least the packs of paparazzi that stalked the couple across two continents had now disappeared, much to her relief. 'People don't recognise me now,' she admitted. 'It was different when I was living with Heath.'

CHAPTER 10

A GRIMM LIFE

If Heath's private life during 2003 and 2004 had been eventful in no way did this affect his film productivity during that time – quite the opposite, he was constantly flying around the world to take part in a remarkably wide range of productions.

Soon after meeting with Naomi Watts on the *Ned Kelly* set he was off to Prague again, this time to co-star in *The Brothers Grimm*, a fantasy film based on the lives of German brothers Jacob and Wilhelm, who collected and published European folk-tales in the early 19th century, which thrilled – and frightened – generations of children during the subsequent 200 years. *Snow White*, *Cinderella*, *Little Red Riding Hood*, *Rapunzel* and *Hansel and Gretel* were among the classics chronicled in their books.

It was far from a normal film biography, however. Given the director in charge of the project it could hardly be anything less than unusual. The man behind the camera as filming began in late summer 2003 was former *Monty Python* member Terry Gilliam. Heath excitedly said, 'I'm a huge fan of Terry's work and I've always been a *Monty Python* fan,' adding, 'We kind of brought a bit of Baron Munchausen-esque humour into it,' with a reference to one of Gilliam's earlier films.

He couldn't compare *The Brothers Grimm* with any recent work from the director's catalogue, however, as the Prague-based film was due to be his first release since the end of the 1990s. Following his days as animator in the Python television shows and films, Gilliam had built a reputation for being one of the most innovative directors around, but his films had a history of being anything but predictable and on occasions, plagued by off-camera problems. His credits included directing or co-directing two *Monty Python* films and such weird extravaganzas as *Time Bandits*, *Jabberwocky*, *The Adventures of Baron Munchausen* and the highly-praised *Brazil*.

In between this list were a number of ideas that never came to fruition and, most famously, the film that accounted for that lull after 1998's *Fear and Loathing in Las Vegas* starring Johnny Depp. For years Gilliam had wanted to make a film based on Don Quixote, the fabled Spanish fictional hero who travelled the land 'tilting at windmills' in his quest for truth and honour. The resulting £32-million *The Man Who Killed Don Quixote* collapsed due to the illness of the leading actor, Jean Rochefort, at the start of shooting and catastrophic weather that washed away the entire set. The project, which again had Depp on board, was scrapped and the nightmare subsequently captured in the documentary *Lost in La Mancha*.

All that was hopefully behind Gilliam, however, when shooting started in Prague, with Heath as Jacob (or 'Jake' as he was called in the film), and *Bourne Identity* star Matt Damon as Wilhelm ('Will', as he was referred to). Being a Terry Gilliam project this was never going to be an ordinary biography. His vision of the brothers transformed them from the linguist researchers they had been in real life into a pair of 19th-century conmen, who duped people into paying them to drive out 'evil creatures' that are, in reality, fake beings created by the pair themselves.

Eventually the two are asked by the French government to deal with a 'real' evil creature – played by Monica Bellucci – that sends them off on a wild adventure. Heath and Matt Damon, it should be emphasised, were two of the biggest young 'hunks' in cinema, yet it was hard to recognise them in their Bavarian costumes and make-up. Heath's hair was cropped and he wore a pair of spectacles perched on the end of his nose. And talking of noses, the entire film almost came to nought in a row over Matt Damon's false nose. *The Times* of London was among the newspapers later to report that Gilliam clashed with the film backers Bob and Harvey Weinstein over the false nose that the director wanted to put on Damon. *The Times* reported that:

The director believed that Damon, who plays one of a pair of conmen who extort money from villagers by eradicating fairytale villains of their own creation, had too cute a nose for his part. He persuaded the actor to add a bump to his snout, which transformed his appearance. 'It actually changed him,' Gilliam said. 'It was like Dumbo and his feather. Matt walked different. He behaved different. Girls looked at him differently. He looked like a young Marlon Brando.' The Weinsteins thought otherwise. On the night before shooting was scheduled to begin they contacted Gilliam. 'They came over and said: "We close the film down if you put the bump on his nose," Gilliam said, 'That is the madness: [there is] this huge juggernaut of a movie roaring down the road and there's this little nose in the middle.' He capitulated, but it was his biggest regret. 'I wake up in the middle of the night wondering what would have happened if I had just secretly put that bump back.'

Bob Weinstein said he was mystified by Gilliam's reaction: 'Any film involves the making of 10,000 decisions. If you only concentrate on the few we had issues with, you ignore the 9,997 we left totally to Terry... I didn't think we should fix a nose on Matt Damon because people are used to looking at him as he is. I told Terry it would be the most expensive nose job in history.'

Gilliam, who was also upset over the Weinstein brothers' objection to his original choice of leading lady, even considered walking out of the project but was persuaded that had he won the ensuing legal battle, he would still spend a year in and out of the courts. Five weeks later, he thought about leaving again. Bob Weinstein personally fired his director of photography, Nicola Pecorini, allegedly for shooting too slowly: 'At that point I said: "All right, I will finish the film on one condition. We will not speak again."' He added that he was one of a club of directors who would never work with the Weinsteins again: 'I like to think of them as a once-in-a-lifetime experience. Some people can deal with them and others can't deal with them so well. They are passionate; that is both the good and bad thing.'

Bob Weinstein again had a different interpretation of events: 'We felt that Nicola was slow, and we fired him to avoid a $75-million movie turning into a $90-million movie.' Gilliam went back to work, but of own admission he walked around the set at times muttering, 'Why the f**k am I doing this movie?'

When the film was eventually released a year later than planned after various alterations were made, he said he was talking to the Weinsteins again, although he considered he had lost his 'fight' with them. 'I'm used to riding roughshod over studio executives, but I couldn't do that with the Weinsteins,' he confessed. The tension between the director and the men financing the film could be detected in an interview Gilliam gave to *Time* magazine, in which he stated, 'You know, of course, what the real issue is here: it's $80 million. When a company puts up $80 million to make a movie, they have come to expect to get what they pay for, and what they want to pay for, generally, is a movie that bears a great resemblance to whatever the last movie was that made them enormous amounts of profit. Whereas, if I receive $80 million, especially from someone who has actually taken the time to watch my previous films, I have to assume they would want me to make something that film-goers haven't just been bored beyond belief by. Not something avant-garde or even terribly original, for that matter, just something different.

'You know what my problem is?' he asked rhetorically. 'I'm a silly, silly optimist. I think it's all so obvious everyone will understand what we're out to accomplish. Which is to do something a bit different, not start a revolution.' As Heath pithily put it: 'There was never a dull moment on the set.' At least he was seeing eye-to-eye with his director even if others weren't: 'When I get nervous my hands go "Waaah... Rrrrr,"' said Heath, flailing his arms about when asked on set how he got on with Gilliam. 'Everything inside me goes at a hundred miles an hour. Usually when I'm working it's, "OK, I'm going to centre myself." But Terry says, "I love all this stuff you do. Just go for it." So he's provoked a lot of my stupidity,' adding, 'He's an incredible, dignified, intellectual visualist, and as mad as a mongoose.'

Perhaps it was the 'mongoose' in Gilliam that meant it was not until the summer of 2005, two years after Heath had started filming, that the movie was released. The director was to comment to the *Guardian* newspaper in England that he was confident that the Weinsteins, despite the differences that had been encountered, would 'sell the s**t out of it, and make it a success. They're the best at it!'

He added, 'As I said to Bob [Weinstein], this may not be a good marriage, because they are who they are, and I am who I am, and we just may not manage to get through this thing. It was about perception, really – different views of what the film should be. I can only do what I do; I don't know how to do anything else. They do what they do; there is no middle position. It was crazy. The worst thing you can do is compromise, then everyone loses that way.'

Gilliam even went off and made another film, *Tideland*, before returning to the editing process on *The Brothers Grimm*: 'The six-month hiatus was good for everybody. I saw a couple of things I could change. You know what I did? I cut out the most expensive scene in the movie. It was something I'd thought about, but didn't have the balls to do until I'd walked away from it for a bit. It'll be on the DVD – the most expensive extra ever made. It's a great sequence, a fight in a tree. But Terry Jones [one of the Python gang] spotted the problem. It made the movie broken-backed. It happens in the middle of the story and, as it's the most spectacular bit, where can you go after that? To cut out the most expensive scene, that was difficult. But at least we all came out liking the movie.' He also added dryly: 'Everybody's happy now. We're a big happy family… there's a good side and a bad side about working with the Weinsteins. They're like old-fashioned studio heads, not bureaucrats. I told Harvey I really admire what they do. I like watching them work – from a long distance away.'

By early spring Heath was back in Los Angeles ready to start on what was, strangely, the first film he had ever made in LA since moving to the city 7 years earlier. 'It's the first job in my career where I can finish work and go home. When you rarely get a chance to be at home, that's what you want. You want stability, your sofa,' said Heath, who was still living with Naomi Watts at the time.

The Lords of Dogtown was to be directed by Catherine Hardwicke, whose first film, *Thirteen*, caused controversy with its depiction of the sex lives of very young teenagers, as well as showing drug and alcohol abuse among them. Her new film was based on a documentary, *Dogtown and Z-Boys*, which told the story of how a bunch of disaffected 1970s' young surfers from the run-down area of Santa Monica in California, known as 'Dogtown', became famous for their skateboarding skills. Heath played Skip Engblom, who guided the youngsters to success. As well as enabling him to work in his hometown for the first time, the film also meant that he could show off the surfing skills learnt years before while growing up in Perth: 'I've been out there most mornings in Venice and up at Point Doom, which is like a private beach up there.' He was also doing a lot of skateboarding during filming and he considered that he was coping with that too: 'I'm OK. The tip is, "Stay on, don't fall off!"'

'I got my first skateboard, designed by one of the Z-boys, Stacy Peralta, when I was about 12. I was a surfer too, because if you lived where I did in Australia, you had to surf or you didn't fit in. I read *Skateboarder* magazine and all these magazines that the Z-boys were always in, so I knew a lot about them. And then I saw the documentary,

Dogtown and Z-Boys, which I loved. After that I felt like they were my family. These days I surf near my home in Bronte when I'm in Sydney and I go down to Venice Beach in LA, but the water is so dirty there. The surfing and skate culture is such a universal thing – like in the way you communicate and the way you are.'

Engblom, he said, 'was a bit of a father figure, maybe more of a Faginesque kind of figure. But Skip did genuinely care for these kids who had rough home lives and lived to surf at the Pacific Ocean Park Pier. They needed help and a direction in life. Engblom gave it to them when he introduced them to skateboards with urethane wheels that could cling to the sides of empty swimming pools.' To play Engblom, Ledger had to capture his toothy grin and his strangely nasal drawl: 'I've got such pathetic little wimpish teeth and Skip has such great teeth that I decided I needed a set of fake ones. But then I had to learn how to speak with them because they made me very sibilant and I was whistling all my words.'

Although it was a busy time for him, he had not actually had a film released for a while: 'I sort of took my career and destroyed it,' he commented wryly. 'I had to destroy it in order to rebuild it because I was getting pigeonholed. People weren't giving me a chance to do anything other than be the blond-haired bimbo and it was starting to bore me. I couldn't have spent the rest of my life following the paths that were being presented to me, so I had to start creating some for myself. This year is finally the time that it's coming together for me in terms of testing myself and what I can do:

it's taken a while, but it looks like doors are opening again, and *Lords of Dogtown* is a good beginning.'

He was certainly going to be busy as his hectic 2004 schedule would result in a fine body of work come their 2004/05 release dates. In addition to the filming of *Dogtown*, it was announced he was to star in *Casanova* as the legendary lover, with filming due to start in Venice in late summer and he was also to portray a heroin addict in *Candy*, an Australian film to be shot in Melbourne.

On top of all this he had to do promotional work for *Ned Kelly*, which was soon to open in America. It was a chore he didn't enjoy and he told one interviewer, 'In five years I'll probably still be sitting here, talking to you, publicising some other movie. It's not the worst thing in the world, but probably the worst part of my job.'

His good fortune at being able to work near his home was soon to end, however. By the end of May *Lords of Dogtown* was in the can and he had to pack his bags and head off on location the very next day. The film was one with which he had first been linked some six months earlier when his name was mentioned alongside stars such as Viggo Mortensen and Brad Pitt as being in contention for the leading parts in the movie.

By January 2004 more and more reports quoted 'Hollywood sources', saying that Heath had won one of the main roles. Finally, at the end of January, the *Hollywood Reporter* stated: 'Actors Heath Ledger and Jake Gyllenhaal are to star in an unusual Western in which they play a pair of gay cowboys.' The paper added: 'The movie is based on a short story by *The Shipping News* scribe E. Annie Proulx, and has long been regarded as one of the great screenplays that never got produced.'

The film was to be directed by Taiwanese-born Ang Lee and the story 'revolved around two men who meet one summer in Wyoming and form a bond that spans 20 years.' Heath, whose final split with Naomi Watts had only become public knowledge within the last few days, cannot have guessed as he headed for the airport that his young life was never to be the same again because of the film. It was named after the acclaimed short story from which it was adapted – the movie was titled *Brokeback Mountain*.

CHAPTER 11

BROKEBACK – THE STORY BEGINS

Heath Ledger didn't read the *New Yorker* magazine of 13 October 1997, but in it was a short story that was to change his life. *Brokeback Mountain* by writer E. Annie Proulx, who had already won a Pulitzer Prize for her novel *The Shipping News*, had an immediate impact, gathering universal praise for the already acclaimed writer. Her story detailed the relationship of ranch-hand Ennis Del Mar and rodeo cowboy Jack Twist, who met and fell in love at the fictional Brokeback Mountain in Wyoming in 1963. It then chronicled the life of the men and their affection for each other over the next two decades.

Initially hired to herd sheep across the country, after a bout of drinking one night Jack makes a pass at Ennis, who rejects him at first but then gives way to his advances. Once their work is over, the two men separate and both marry, only to be passionately reunited some years later, agreeing to meet occasionally and go on fishing trips. No fish are caught or sought; instead they revel in each other's company. Over the years both men's marriages deteriorate and eventually Ennis's ends in divorce. Hearing of the break-up, Jack drives to Wyoming in the hope that they can live together at last, only to find that Ennis refuses to move away from his children and is still worried about repercussions if their relationship becomes public knowledge. There are many more twists and turns in the story before its almost inevitable sad conclusion, with the death of Jack.

The roles of Jack and Ennis – characters who some felt might harm a young actor's career – were to bring fame to Jake Gyllenhaal and especially Heath, as the monosyllabic Ennis Del Mar. It is important, therefore, to examine in detail the events that led to the film being made at all and how he came to be chosen for what was undoubtedly his most famous role.

Heath may not have read that original story, but one person who did was the woman eventually to become co-writer of the screenplay, Diana Ossana. One night she was unable to sleep and picked up a copy of the fateful edition of the *New Yorker* that was lying on her bedside table. 'I read the story in the middle of the night and was so moved by it that about two-thirds of the way, I began to sob,' she said. 'It's a love story, a tragic love story, pure and simple. It was like a lightning bolt. I just knew in my gut instinctively that this was something powerful.' She re-read the story the next morning and then enlisted her close friend and fellow writer Larry McMurtry, in whose house she was staying at the time. McMurtry, the writer of *The Last Picture Show* and *Lonesome Dove*, wanted to jointly write the script based on Proulx's short story. 'To say it's a story about gay cowboys is like saying *Lonesome Dove* [the novel that won McMurtry a Pulitzer Prize] is about a cattle drive. We don't consider it a message movie, it just tells a compelling story' Ossana stated simply.

Together, they contacted Annie Proulx and she signed on within a week. 'She only changed one word,' Ossana proudly said. McMurtry was just as keen: 'When I read it the first time I just thought, "Why didn't I write that?" It wasn't regret, it was surprise.'

After obtaining the rights and adapting the story into a screenplay, the pair then faced the problem of finding two actors who would be both fitting for the roles and who would also accept them. 'My cynical view is that we couldn't get the actors because the agencies wouldn't let them go. They thought it would be career suicide,' McMurtry remarked. Several leading directors, including Gus Van Sant and Joel Schumacher, were interested in the script and then finally one came on board who was to see it through to its conclusion: Ang Lee. Born in Taiwan in 1954, by the time *Brokeback Mountain* started shooting in Alberta in the early summer of 2004, he was recognised as one of the finest film-makers of his generation.

Lee came to America in the late 1970s to study film-making. His second film, *The Wedding Banquet*, won him both Oscar and Golden Globe nominations and then *Eat*

Drink Man Woman received a best Foreign Film Oscar nomination. More plaudits came when his first mainstream Hollywood film, *Sense and Sensibility*, was nominated for Best Picture at the Oscars and did indeed win an Oscar for Best Adapted Screenplay for its writer and leading actress, Emma Thompson. In 2000 he made *Crouching Tiger, Hidden Dragon*, which attracted a host of Oscar nominations and won the Best Foreign Language Film award, as well as Best Director at the Golden Globes. Tellingly, it also became the highest grossing foreign-language film ever released in America.

Then came a slight 'blip on the screen' of his career, a multi-million dollar project, *The Hulk*, based on the comic book character of the same name. It was not a success with audiences or critics and Lee even thought briefly about quitting films altogether as a result. He had already read the script of *Brokeback Mountain* before he made *The Hulk* and it was a relief to return to less dollar-intensive films when he decided to proceed with the project.

Lee subsequently told the show-business paper *Variety* about his reasons for making the film and why he chose the two leading actors, both of whom were said to have accepted less than their 'going rate' for the film: 'When I read the short story four years ago, I got choked up. It's just simply a brilliant piece of writing, of great American West literature, a great love story, set in the milieu of a realistic American West. And then it was also a mysterious gay love story. This idea of *Brokeback Mountain*, that the guys spend 20 years chasing after that idea and couldn't get to it, is about the illusion of love. And for me, that's a great ingredient for a love story, but a very strange one. And because of that particularity, it felt very universal.

'And then I went ahead and did *The Hulk*, and I was exhausted. But this story about missing love still haunted me. To balance the film's two elements: the masculine elements of the Western and then the real genre of the film, which is a romantic story and a gay one. Usually in our social and cultural conventions, they're opposing each other, but I had to make them work together, which was the main interest of this particular material. Technically, the hardest thing was the aging. It's a short epic story, only 30 pages long, but it wants you to feel 20 years of epic scope. It surprised me how good the actors were. I deliberately chose younger actors, people under 25, and that innocence goes a long way to the end; it's scary how good they are. One scene that jumps out is the tent scene when they make out for the first time: I think they're very brave, not only with good performances, but they show us private feelings. Usually you don't get that in lovemaking scenes. They take a great risk and the only way to get out of that risk is they have to be really good.'

Lee didn't even audition Ledger for his role. Remarkably the pair never met until after he landed the part. The director explained elsewhere why he made this choice and how *Monster's Ball*, the film Heath only did as a 'favour' after the original actor dropped out, influenced him: 'I knew he was a good actor, particularly from *Monster's*

Ball, he brings so much poetry to the role. He's a great anchor for the movie, a walking poetic cowboy.'

Warming to his theme he continued, 'It's a part of human nature to fear desire and to lose control and so we begin to indulge in self-denial. Self-denial leads to darkness... because it shuts out truth, and then, you have nothing but the darkness and regret, and the memory of what might have been. *Brokeback Mountain* is a romantic symbol of what we fail to attain. It's about loss, it's about fear; it's about the illusory quality of love. Funny how we say people fall in love. We don't walk into love, but we fall. It's this impossible, negative space that we fall into. That's what gives this movie its existential feel because the whole drama takes place in that void... in that negative space, in longing.'

Lee too was moved when he first read the story: 'I cried when I read it. I was interested in directing, but it didn't happen then. I like making dramas about conflict, through which you examine humanity and the complexities of human dynamics. This material was like a goldmine. Maybe as a foreigner, I have a different way of viewing the United States. I don't know... When I make Chinese films, I hear that I am so full of myself. When I do American movies, the first thing they notice is the subtext. Obviously, I twist genre a little bit. But you know, I'm a twisted person in my own mind. In the culture in which I grew up you express yourself indirectly, which is unlike a lot of Western drama, where you get very explicit dramatic scenes where everything is said out loud. We tend to hide behind the scenery, which can then reflect how you feel, and this idea of indirect expression became a very central theme in *Brokeback Mountain* because Jack and Ennis can't talk about what they are feeling.'

Lee's analysis of the story and the film's themes are worth examining in detail because they form an intrinsic part of the '*Brokeback Mountain* phenomenon' and the impact it had on Heath's career. 'I hate calling it a Western movie because I think of Western and I think of gunslingers, it's really more of an epic romance. The story just breaks your heart and it's that sense of loss that connects it to the West – and the loss of the American frontier. You could say there's an almost dirge-like quality to the movie.'

The director said the low budget ($13 million, his lowest in years) and the fact that it was a 'risky' film helped him: 'This is a subject that repulses straight men and so it deals with a lot of repression. *Hulk* was about fear and repression, and the cost of that fear and repression on the individual and society. Ennis has some *Hulk* elements in him because he can be extremely violent – the idea that if you can't fix it then you have to stand it. And sometimes, people can't stand it any longer and they explode. The fact is, people make choices and some of those choices are for self-denial. This movie is about two men and the choices they make. Some might think the idea of the macho man and romance are conflicting, but they aren't. Really, they are two sides of the same coin – one cannot exist without the other – complexity in co-existence. *Brokeback Mountain* let me rediscover the joy of film-making... I can't say I knew what this movie was all about before I started. I had definite ideas, yes, of course, but somehow, that's the truly scary part of making a movie. You don't know what it is – you're in the darkness, and that's my *Brokeback Mountain*.'

But he did admit: 'I thought twice about it. It didn't make sense why anybody would make this movie. The place you don't know, the gayness you don't know; it's so hard it wrenches your guts. *The Hulk* really beat me. It was a huge budget with all the pressure from the first weekend and it got to me. I felt very much alone. I needed a movie to get me out of my depression. This was a healing process for me.'

He expanded his views in a question-and-answer session with the *Oregonian* newspaper, in which he said: 'This is really a love story set in the real West, which overlaps with the Western quite a bit but isn't the same. I think the Western is an invented genre in the movies. It's like a martial arts film: a movie genre. But this is quite different. There are a lot of Western elements that have a lot of cultural implications, which aren't really what this movie is about. The masculinity is there. And the post-Western tradition which I found in some Sam Peckinpah movies – that elegiac feeling. That's very popular in Western literature. It's spare and poetic and colourful. So that's great for our movie. The cinematography, the music: it all carries that tone, which comes from the writing. The landscapes have a long history from the art of the West: painting and still photography and literature. And Larry

McMurtry told me about how the Western establishment worked from the end of the Civil War to the turn of the century and how it disappeared. That's where that elegiac, melancholy mood comes from.

'And underneath the love story, that's what you have to work with. The myth of the West inspired these boys to their work. But they just do ranch work, hard work. They don't know why the West has died or why the cowboy world disappeared. The business is gone, but they still believe in the myth and that's a great environment for a poignant love story like this.'

He was then asked: 'Of the two characters Heath Ledger's seemed to me the more traditional Western type: taciturn, reserved, kind of like Gary Cooper. What sort of discussions did you have with him about that?' To which he replied, 'It was a long process for us to get into that character. It's a nonverbal culture so we had to develop his body language which keeps the viewer – and Jack – in the distance, but not too far away, because he needs him. And that's a skill we developed in the rehearsal period. He doesn't talk like that so we found a real person that he took that from. They do chew and bite their lips like that in Wyoming. You have that lazy tongue thing, too. So putting that together was making him hard to read but that's his character. Jake Gyllenhaal didn't do that; his character wasn't like that – he's a salesman and a romantic. But Heath is more anchored to that melancholy mood of the West.'

The question of the 'ageing' of the actors during the 20-year time span of the film was also raised. Lee responded:

'Subtle changes in age are harder than if you make them 90 years old. Not only from end to end but from scene to scene; there's two or three years between scenes and the change is rather subtle. Technically, that was the hardest thing to do in this movie: to show the ageing in hair, make-up, costume, facial hair, lighting… But they have to carry more than half of the job. The way they carry themselves and the way they voice themselves. We had to make a chart and screen tests and stick to that because we were shooting out of order. The budget was about $13 million or so and we couldn't afford it.' But he added, 'After struggling with two big movies before this I was very happy to be on this set because the production was relatively easy for me. I decided that because of the budget and the nature of the film it had to be shot in a very simple way. So getting the actors right was most of it, and shooting was relatively easy and I just had a great time.'

As mentioned, one of the key moments in the story is when Ennis and Jack first make love in their tiny tent on the mountainside. Although only on-screen for a short time, it is central to the entire theme. Lee explained how he handled the making of this scene, which was shot no less than 13 times, and its two young, heterosexual stars: 'Before you go about those scenes you get worked up, thinking it's not going to be easy. You prepare this way and that way. And when you actually shoot them it can be quite easy just to get it done. The most challenging for me was the scene in the tent, the first make-out scene. Basically I just rolled camera; we didn't know what we wanted to get.

We just rehearsed them by talking through it and how it fits in the overall development. On the day, we blocked the scene and got the idea of what we were getting into. And I blocked in a cold tone and rolled the cameras just expecting them to deliver it – and they did.

'I'm a shy guy, and that's usually how I go about lovemaking scenes – just explain it technically and talk out my feelings and then just go for it. Once they start, it's easy to talk about. Blocking gives them a good idea of what you're after, what's important. I don't storyboard. When I tell them what has to be done step-by-step, they're good actors, they know what acts reflect what meanings; they're experienced. They know that certain acts mean temptation or distance or confusion. I respect their privacy and I don't think I need to tell them more than what is needed.' Elsewhere he said, 'I tried to shoot very quickly and used simple film language.'

He chose a location near Calgary in Alberta, Canada, instead of Wyoming as it was less expensive to film there, but apart from that the director insisted on total authenticity. He studied up on cowboy culture with the help of both Proulx, who gave him a tour of north-east Wyoming, where she lives, and McMurtry, who showed him around ranches in his native Texas. These were not one-way conversations, though: 'Because they know Westerns so well, Larry and Diana often take the genre for granted,' explains Lee. 'For example, neither the story nor the first script had a second lovemaking scene, which I thought was necessary in order to understand why they keep wanting to go back for the next 20 years. The first time they are in the tent, it's almost like a mishap. But then they have to consciously commit to it, and that should be tender and sexy.'

It was remarkable that Heath had not met his director before being cast in such a central role: 'He just struck me as a good cowboy and his face is easy to photograph. It's hard to describe – when you rest a movie on someone, it's always a gamble, especially when they're not a big movie star.'

It is important to bear in mind all that Lee has to say about the film in general and Heath in particular for a very simple reason: without doubt *Brokeback Mountain* is *the* film for which Heath Ledger will be best remembered, guaranteeing him a place in Hollywood's hall of fame. Lee's vision and the way in which Heath holds it together are so entwined as to be inseparable. The director summed up his views on the film's leading characters and their screen wives – and the actors who played them – in the following succinct manner:

Heath as Ennis: 'He grew up on the Australian range and knows ranch work. I was impressed with him in *Monster's Ball*, but he wasn't a leading man, so I decided to take a risk. Heath is a good anchor for the movie. He adds to that brooding, nonverbal, elegiac mood.'

Jake Gyllenhaal as Jack: 'Jake's unlike a typical cowboy and unlike the way Jack is in the short story.

He's more positive, romantic, bright – an adventurer. He's also a great young actor. The two main characters should have great chemistry so playing Jake opposite Heath was a good choice.'

Michelle Williams, who played Ennis's wife Alma: 'She was the first one at the casting session. As soon as she walked in, I just believed she was Alma. I first noticed her in *The Station Agent*; I'd never seen her TV work. The way she acts is very genuine and believable, like a child-actor, but more sophisticated and experienced.'

Anne Hathaway as Jack's wife Lureen: 'Anne came in with her hair and make-up done – she was shooting *The Princess Diaries 2* on the same lot. We had her read the scene with Heath on the phone, which is heavy-duty. Again, I didn't see *The Princess Diaries* – her reading sold me. It's scary how good she is.'

But what of the two leading actors who risked alienating their fan base with their performances? First, Jake Gyllenhaal – already established through films such as *Donnie Darko* and *The Day After Tomorrow* – who initially became aware of *Brokeback* when Gus Van Sant was pencilled in to direct. At first he wanted nothing to do with it: 'I was like, "No way!" At 18 years old, it's not something you want to be involved in. Five years later I read the script, knowing Ang was directing and I just had to do it. There was no hesitation, there really wasn't. When you know you have someone who's made movies that deal with pretty challenging themes and has tackled them with the kind of universality and compassion that Ang has, you throw yourselves into the arms of that person and you trust them and you feel safe and you go for it. It's not like it didn't go through my mind that people were going to have big problems with it but sometimes something comes along and I just lock on to it and say, "Take me for the ride! That gives me oxygen to breathe!" I didn't really think, "Oh, I'm going to have to make out with Heath Ledger."'

He told the *Los Angeles Daily News*: 'I would not want to be in a movie that didn't stir up people's opinions. The only problem I have is when people make opinions before they've seen something. Judgement before experience is something that is a fault of mine and a fault of a lot of people that I know and I do not think it's a good thing in myself. When people see these movies, they'll see what they're about. But yeah, after they see them, they may have opinions. Did it change my perspective on gay cowboys? It's very hard to make this movie experience into a literal one. It's about the struggles of two people dealing with intimacy, to me. You don't have this ideal idea of love like you see in movies all the time, that thing like: it's supposed to happen between these two people, particularly a guy and a girl – and when he gets the girl at the end, the whole thing is all good. But this puts it in an environment where we've never seen it before. I think you walk out of this film feeling devastated in a lot of ways – but also feeling a real sense of benevolence.'

Gyllenhaal was realistic enough to know that most

people wanted to ask him about the love scenes with Heath: 'What I'm really interested in is why so many people are interested in how different it is – and most of them are men! But I can't really tell you, except to say that it was an exfoliating experience and one that I will do to service a film, maybe, but definitely not in my real life. We didn't really rehearse it at all. We talked about it, I guess, a little bit. But on the day, there was a lot of choreography. It was a lot like whenever I'm doing a love scene with a woman in a movie. They have a particularly hard time not being objectified so when you're working with them, it's always like, "I'm gonna put my hand here, I'm gonna go here..." It was very much the same thing. I think both Heath and I have worked with women in the past like that, so we worked with each other that way... It was like a dance, you know? The difference between a best friend and a soul mate is the difference of consummating it or not. Once you see the two of them do it, the friendship that they have together and the things that they share together – and the fun that they have with each other – is kind of easy, especially being two straight guys. I think that we have a chemistry just as friends and I think that we dove into the love scenes – and then jumped out as fast as we could.'

In one highly charged scene, Ennis greets Jack four years after their first meeting. He grabs him and kisses him passionately against a wall: 'Heath almost broke my nose in a scene. He grabs me and he slams me up against the wall and kisses me. And then I grab him and I slam him up against the wall and I kiss him. And we were doing take after take, after take.'

So what did Heath make of all this? Strong as Gyllenhaal's performance undoubtedly was, it is Heath's Ennis Del Mar that holds the entire film together. Unable to leave his commitments and fearing the hostility and antagonism of family and friends, he refuses to accept his one chance of true happiness with the more-willing Jack Twist. Ennis is the ultimate Marlboro Man, with his practically inarticulate response to the most extreme of emotions. All these were conveyed by Heath, who even trained with weights to 'bulk' him up for the role in a way that surprised many of his most fervent admirers.

After filming was completed he discussed, in various conversations with interviewers and friends, the challenge of the role and how he approached it. It is necessary to examine his thought process in detail to understand his approach to the part and how essential that was in the 'end product' – one of the finest performances in the history of film. 'I would have been crazy to turn it down,' he admitted, 'any anxiety toward doing it was manufactured through the industry. It obviously wasn't as big a deal for us, because we did it. I think the chemistry was on the page, in the words… We just had to portray it… The whole shooting experience for me was incredibly lonely. Whether or not Ang created that environment for me to work and live in or I created it for myself – it's a lonely story so it's hard not to take it home with you and feel lonely. If it was in anybody's else's hands I probably wouldn't have made the movie but it was Ang Lee, who's a genius and who I consider the perfect director for it. And the material itself – there was no reason to worry about it because it was one of the most beautiful screenplays I've ever read. So all the elements were there... It was pretty much a perfect set-up. You'd be an idiot to walk away from it.

'All I could think was that it was the best script I'd ever been offered. Apart from that, it put the fear of God into me. It was not the kind of thing I was going to ask my agent to get for me. I looked at the story and thought, "Never mind the sex – how am I going to look into Jake's eyes convincingly, with love?" That was going to be a huge challenge. The complexity of the character in the end made me want to take this chance. I was fascinated with how Ennis was struggling with his own views and personal emotions. I have read a lot of scripts about love and quite honestly, we have seen them and heard them all before. But this was a beautiful, complex story – and a true story of love. I am just hoping audiences will come along and think, "We have not seen anything like this before." That is what I was trying to achieve. And I feel, when I really think about it, that is why I became involved in the first place. The risk, for me, was not in playing Ennis, it was in turning the role down.'

He admitted that both he and Gyllenhaal were 'very, very nervous' about the gay love scene: 'It's not something that we'd searched for in everyday life. But we're pretty sensible people, Jake and I. We realised we're just two people; we realised it's necessary for the story. The level of intimacy had to be portrayed to increase the level of heartache for the story. It's easy to say it was difficult and hard, but it's really awkward having to do a love scene with anyone – whether it's a guy or a girl. There's a guy with the boom standing over you. It's always awkward. I never thought twice about it. For one thing, I never felt like I had anything at stake and I think if you make decisions based on society's opinions, you're going to make boring choices.

'What terrified me was self-doubt. I knew that if I was going to do justice to this character, to this story and to this form of love, I was really going to have to mature as an actor and as a person. Look, everyone wants me to go, "Yes, it was difficult and horrible and the worst thing you could do," but at the end of the day, it was just kissing a human being. The first take was a little awkward – it was new territory, so to speak – but afterward it was, "Get on with the job."

'For me it was a little easier than it was for Jake... Any kind of nerves I had about approaching that scene, I didn't have to hide. We were like, "F**k it, we took on this story and there's no point in shying away from it." Neither of us wanted to do it again any time soon. But in the end, it was just like kissing a person. Most of my preparation was in finding the voice so that with the accent, I could find his soul. A lot of my time [also] went into trying to represent his inner battle through his posture or lack of posture, both physically and emotionally. That was the challenge for me – and hardening myself. It's a part of human nature to fear desire and to lose control and so we begin to indulge in self-denial. Self-denial leads to darkness... because it shuts out truth and then you have nothing but the darkness and regret and the memory of what might have been. *Brokeback Mountain* is a romantic symbol of what we fail to attain. It's about loss, it's about fear; it's about the illusory quality of love. I have a kind of frantic and nervous energy and I thought that would be my biggest battle, trying to stay still. But once we got out to the wilderness and were surrounded by those mountains and rivers and trees, you truly become a product of the environment. That's what I wanted – and then the stillness just came quite naturally.'

At the 2005 Toronto Film Festival he spoke at length about the film: 'I never went to acting school or had any classes... All of my mistakes are on film. In other words, it's been a long, slow process in discovering how to act and I'm still figuring it out. I guess in the past I never felt like I was ready; I never felt like I deserved the career that was somewhat handed to me on a platter at an early age. I didn't want to take the shortcut route. I wanted to take the route where I had to struggle a little. In doing so, you mature as a person.

'When you mature as a person, you mature as an actor; it goes hand in hand. In the last couple of years, I wanted to pull out all of the stuff that was locked inside of me and go for it. I wanted to find out what Ennis was battling inside. The conclusion I came to is that he was battling his genetic structure. He was fighting the traditions and values, and fears and ideals that had been passed down to him through his father. Also, what does being trapped (gay man in a superstraight world) do to your voice? Your voice must have a battle of its own. Each word has to kind of punch its way out, to fight its way out. Expression is a fight for Ennis. I wanted to try to find a voice for him, a way of moving his mouth. I wanted sounds to be too loud for him, the lights to be too bright for him. Any form of expression was overload. You find all that stuff and (the performance) falls into place.

'Then, of course, there's the stillness. I think that's a real trait in anyone who spends a lot of time isolated out in the middle of Mother Nature, the Rocky Mountains. You become a product of your environment. I wanted Ennis to blend into his environment; I wanted him to be a rock. That was kind of the point. I wanted to create the most masculine character I'd played to date but love transcends all shapes and sizes. I had a dear friend of mine, who's my "uncle." He's the head of the Australian arm-wrestling federation. He's a big guy – he goes to bare-knuckle fighting out in the Nevada desert and he's gay. I think sometimes that the toughness can be a direct compensation for the way we all perceive them; it's overcompensating. I don't think *Brokeback Mountain* is a story about overcompensation, it's just the way these guys are. Ranch hands are fairly rugged people. It just happens to be that two souls within these vessels fall in love. I definitely knew it was going to take courage, but that was what was alluring about the project for me. I knew it would be rewarding in terms of what I'd learn about acting.

'It's so easy in this industry to keep playing safe and do stuff that doesn't test you. You can sit on a plâteau and do the easy stuff. It felt like we were all in the same position. I'm an Australian telling an American story, playing a ranch hand from Wyoming. Ang is obviously an outsider to American culture as well – he didn't grow up here. He had to investigate, to discover the story... It wasn't coming from within him. He's a tough man to work for, he's very shy on compliments... You always walk away at the end of the day feeling like you underachieved and so you want to come back the next day and push it to a higher level. My character is very afraid of offending or hurting anyone. It's my first nature, probably, to avoid confrontation. But I do like to challenge, to examine conflict – inner conflict, particularly. You have to go there to examine humanity. Otherwise, we cover ourselves up. I knew I had to age convincingly. I relied on hair and make-up, dropping my voice and a few movements but it was not easy. Working with Ang Lee in the hardest conditions – and God, it was cold and bleak up there – made me feel like years were going past, rather than months.'

In one live television interview he gave a fascinating insight into Lee's work process when asked about the mechanics of the filming: 'Actually there are two sections to Ang's directing, I found – certainly on this film – and there's the pre-production side of Ang, which was the information was incredibly thorough, you know, and he, you know, it was more personal, like his direction, like he took us aside individually and gave us an insight into his

HEATH LEDGER

observations and his personal objectives to the film and the story and our characters.'

Interviewer: 'What did he say?'

Heath: 'Oh well, you know, it was always – whenever Ang does speak – certainly during this time it was always very few words and it was always very profound, somewhat poetic little statements that somehow made complete sense, you know, perfect sense. I think one of the things he focused in on me is, obviously, you can see me sitting here when I'm nervous, my hands are going everywhere, and it's very hard for me to stay still. And I'm even like that kind of in the rehearsal process, I'm kind of spitting out my words. And Ang would just, I think, he saw that in me and would just keep on repeating, "Stillness, stillness, stillness." And so I was like, OK, well, this is obviously my weakness, you know, on this job and I took that away. There were obviously many other things. But then, you know, the stillness actually ended up being one of the easiest sides of this job once I got out into the wilderness and amongst these majestic mountainsides and rivers and trees, and you know, you truly become a product of your environment. And so the stillness just kind of happened.

'And so that's one side of him in the pre-production – and it truly is thorough and he gives us a lot of information. We go away, digest it, process it and kind of create our own characters. And also in that process was the acting. You know, it was a big part of it – finding his voice, finding the correct regional accent and then kind of

174

characterising the accent, you know, because Ennis had such a – his inabilities to express, I wanted to kind of, you know, I wanted him to be a clenched fist because any form of expression had to be painful. And my mouth I wanted to be a clenched fist as well and therefore any word, words that escaped from within had to kind of fight their way out. And so that was one side. That was the pre-production. And then the other side was the shooting, the direction throughout the actual shooting process. And when it got to making the film everything just went silent and still.

'There were very – there was very little direction from him directly to us. It was almost as if, you know, we got to witness – it was very clear that the film – the shooting side of the film – this was now his time to create. And if we hadn't done our homework and hadn't prepared and created characters from his notes and from the short story, from the script, then we were just – you know, it was bad casting.'

He was to later say, 'I had a dialect coach, of course, because it's a very particular accent. In terms of capturing the ranch hand from Middle America, it's like surfers, in France or American or anywhere else, they all say "Dude" and look at life in the same way. I grew up in Perth, Western Australia, and we had many people similar to Ennis in the way he walks and talks, and spits and smokes. It's very similar to the American way.'

Even during filming that summer and autumn of 2004 there was a 'buzz' about the film and the impact it would have when released. No one could quite have anticipated the astonishing reaction that lay ahead, however.

Heath probably would not have had too much time to ponder what lay ahead. As well as being busy with filming he had other things on his mind; he was falling madly in love with his screen wife, actress Michelle Williams.

CHAPTER 12

LOVE ON THE SET

Midway through *Brokeback Mountain* there is a scene where Heath as 'happily married man' Ennis del Mar is tobogganing down a hillside with his wife, years before their relationship is torn apart. The couple fall off and roll about laughing in the snow, a picture of domestic bliss. Ennis and Alma (played by Michelle Williams) look very young and very much in love. So they should – for the two stars were already in the early stages of a romance as strong as any that was being depicted on screen.

Michelle actually hurt her knee during later takes of the scene and Heath was so concerned that he scurried around her for days afterwards, caring and supportive as she struggled with the discomfort caused by the fall.

The scene was one of the very first to be shot and had to be done in May 2004, early on in the film schedule, to capture the snow remaining on the hillside before it disappeared under the summer sun. Even at such a formative stage of filming, the signs were there for all to see: the pair was very much 'an item.'

'We were knee-deep in snow and on the fifth take, Michelle and I were tobogganing down the hill – we were supposed to fall off, having a fun time. But Michelle was screaming in pain. She'd twisted her knee – she was pretty much on crutches for the rest of the shoot. And I felt I always had to look after her after that,' recalled Heath. 'The whole thing was astonishing. My relationship with Michelle was something that slowly fell into place; we were just like two peas in a pod.'

Ang Lee had enough on his mind in his role of director, but he immediately noticed the spark between the young couple and thought, 'Does he have a lady thing with her?'

It quickly became clear that Michelle had damaged her knee ligaments and she was unable to stand because of the immense pain. Heath remained by her side, comforting her, and when an ambulance arrived to take her for treatment he insisted on riding with her. 'Heath was all worked up and holding her hands and wanted to go to hospital,' Lee said. That was when the film crew had their first suspicions there was love in the air, although the attraction had been there from the start.

Not that Lee objected to the relationship or feared that it might impair Heath's performance: 'It was really good for Heath. The character is very intense and has a lot of self-loathing, a lot of vulnerability, and the nourishment of the love affair and happiness kept him grounded. Did it distract him from playing a gay cowboy? I think it's just the opposite, because he's so secure and happy that he really focused on his work.'

Jake Gyllenhaal too noticed the attraction straightaway: 'I remember being at rehearsal and the two of them being googly-eyed looking at each other. I left for two weeks and came back and they were in love. We were all living in trailers while we were shooting the movie. There were four trailers and there quickly became three.'

Gyllenhaal's screen wife Ann Hathaway had an even crisper summary of Heath and Michelle's love: 'There were sparks immediately, there totally were. The first day I was there we were all sitting having lunch together. Michelle had hurt her knee and Heath was playing with her crutches. Every once in a while Heath would look up and she would look up... I'm sorry, it was just adorable.'

So, who was the girl who captured Heath's heart on that snow-kissed mountainside?

Twenty-three at the time she met Heath, Michelle Williams was the eldest of 5 children from, coincidentally, the cowboy country of Montana. A child actor from the age of 8, with appearances in commercials for fabric softener and pizzas, followed by parts in television shows such as *Lassie*, *Baywatch* and *Home Improvement*, she was cast in one of the leading roles in *Dawson's Creek*, which could well be described as an American version of one of Heath's Australian television series, *Home and Away*. *Dawson's Creek* was a massive success and she played Jen Lindley for all 6 seasons of the show, becoming recognised by a large young audience through the role.

But it wasn't Williams' acting in *Dawson's Creek* that caught Ang Lee's eye when he was casting for *Brokeback Mountain* – he had not even seen one episode of the show. Instead it was her role in a low-key minor hit film called *The Station Agent* in 2003, about a dwarf who inherits an isolated, abandoned railway station, for which she and the rest of the cast were nominated for a Screen Actors' Guild nomination for Best Acting Ensemble. Michelle flew to Los Angeles from New York to read for the role in front of Ang Lee: 'I felt strangely calm that day and did everything I wanted to do and left feeling really peaceful. I don't know if in retrospect it felt destined, but it felt really nice.'

It felt 'nice' for Ang Lee too: 'I only knew her from *The Station Agent*. She just felt like there was something different, genuine. And then I met her and as soon as she walked in, I knew – she was so natural and real.'

Williams got the part and that brought her into Heath's life.

'Heath and I were a good support for each other outside of the filming,' she said. 'I remember us being so exhausted at the end of a day and just sitting over a dinner table with him and commiserating, or just taking it easy together because the days and nights were really long and really gruelling – and really sad.'

There was never a danger that she might confuse the reality of her love for Heath with her screen character's feelings for Ennis, however: 'They feel like such truly separate experiences, working together and then not working together... the two didn't really meet. I feel like they existed on separate time planes.'

Heath recalled one early scene with Michelle and discussing with her how they would approach it: 'I remember sitting in the trailer with Michelle, talking and playing cards, trying to figure out what we were going to do. And then Ang walks past the door. And he says to us, "Ha! Ha! Ha! Very hard scene! Ha! Ha! First day. Very hard scene! Ha! Ha! Ha! Ha! Ha!" And then Ang walks off, kind of laughing to himself. And we look out the trailer. And he's still laughing at the fact that he'd just thrown us in the deep end – and he did. But it forced us into figuring out our entire stories because we were suddenly thrown into the 40-year-old end of our characters and we had to figure out everything that happened beforehand very quickly. She is beautiful, she's gorgeous and I'm so proud of her in this film. She is an incredibly talented actor and she really shines in this movie – I think she gives the best performance in the film. I'm incredibly proud of her.'

Michelle had her own views on her character, Alma: 'She loves him in the way that it is so easy to love somebody who is so clearly wrong for you. That's the primary reason she stays – she loves him and she is not willing to let go so easily of this ideal.'

Although the film is set in 1960s Wyoming, Williams knew something of the small-town mentality from her early childhood in Montana: 'I recognised a lot of it. Of course, the landscape and the effect that living on a terrain like that can have on one's psyche, I understand that really well from watching generations of my family farm. I knew a lot about Alma instantly. She was the person I loved when I read the script. The love story between the two men is very strong, but my eyes went to Alma – she was where my heart was. But there were always adjustments to be made on set, by me and by Ang, and things I had to go further with. Because Alma's not me, and I've never really known anybody who's exactly like her, there was a lot of imagination and research that went into her that should always be a part of the process. I understand what living in that kind of climate and environment does to a person, what living that kind of life looks like on a person's face and in their body over an extended period of time. I've seen it in my great-grandparents, my grandparents and my parents. We left Montana when I was 8 or 9, so I had to go beyond that – I had to contemporise my view of things. But it gave me something deep in my bones.'

One of the most paradoxical parts of the filming was that as Heath and Michelle grew close in real life, their screen counterparts were drifting further away from each other. But she never felt any confusion or clash between the two situations: 'It felt so separate. I, Michelle, wasn't hurt in those scenes in which Heath's character was moving away from me. It was lonely to be Alma, to be married to Ennis, but I didn't ever confuse the two. Our feelings about each other are very clear: I never got tripped up.'

Although the film is primarily about Ennis' and Jack's

love for each other, both the 'wife' roles have great substance. They seem to form a part of the greater narrative rather than merely sub-plots. This meant Michelle took part in two of the strongest scenes. In one she catches a glimpse out of the window of Ennis greeting Jack with a passionate body-shaking kiss after a four-year absence: 'I remember preparing for that scene,' Michelle told *Interview* magazine. 'I was all alone. There was nobody in the apartment. I had this little corridor all to myself to prepare in and I remember just tiptoeing in the space and trying to go as lightly and as sensitively as I possibly could. I wanted to be like water, to be able to pass through your fingers. Ah, it was really sensitive, delicate, hocus-pocus kind of work that I was trying to do. And you know what? I don't know if it was me or if it was the character, but it sent pins through my heart to open the door because I wasn't preparing myself to see them do that; I was preparing myself for unexpectedness.'

In another scene Ennis has sex with her roughly, as if she was Jack. 'I felt everything Alma would have,' she added. 'Demoralised. Unsexy. Undesirable. Fatally flawed – and in some pain. But above all, I felt confused. At that point she has an inkling about Ennis and Jack. Things aren't so bad, at least not bad in a public way. She just has suspicions about what happened in the bedroom; that she can handle. I think she can handle almost anything that happens in the sanctity and privacy of her own home. It's the fear of what other people would say and think that drives her out of the marriage. At some point in the movie, Ennis says about the boys' situation, "If you can't fix it, you gotta stand it." I think Alma, too, abides by that sentiment.'

She expanded on her thoughts when she said, 'It feels like the culmination of everything that I've ever wanted or thought about the work that I've done in the past. There's so many reasons, all buried on top of one another, of why she didn't walk out. Initially, she went into a state of shock. You know, those moments when your whole body is shaking and you don't know what you just said. Then, in the long term, why she doesn't confront him – if you've seen the movie, he's a man with violent insides, and I think that she didn't know how to run the risk of endangering herself, him and her two daughters. And then, what would people say? People would find out and the town would talk. Her life would be ruined; her children's lives would be ruined. And all she ever wanted was a husband and two children and an apartment above a laundromat, and I don't think she was that willing to let it go so quickly.'

Heath and Michelle's wasn't the first love ever to blossom on a film set, nor would it be the last. Unlike many such relationships which end with filming, theirs grew stronger, so much so that it was soon public knowledge and they were spotted together on a number of dates around Calgary, simply enjoying each other's company. With his personal life on such an upbeat note, Heath was also busy on the property front. He had spent months looking for an ideal Sydney base and in September moved into a £2 million house in Bayview Street, in the Bronte district of Sydney, named by some as 'the celebrity suburb.' The house, on four levels, overlooked a park and the nearby beach; there were also views from a top-floor Jacuzzi. It had five bedrooms, four bathrooms and two garages, and by the end of the year the couple were living there.

Being back in Sydney did mean he would run into old friends, of course, and on one evening outing to Hugo's restaurant in Bondi the couple bumped into Naomi Watts and some friends. The former lovers chatted for twenty minutes before splitting up. One of the downsides of being in Australia for Heath, however, was not meeting old acquaintances, but his relationship with the press – or to be more accurate some of the paparazzi who were keen to capture lucrative shots of their new hot star. The pressure became even more intense as rumours began to circulate that Michelle might be pregnant.

Heath, who took the unusual step of throwing eggs near them in an attempt to dissuade them, was pretty clear about his attitude to the photographers: 'Some of them swear at you and verbally assault you, even though they don't physically punch you or push you. When someone takes a photo of you and your girlfriend outside your house, it makes you feel like you're being assaulted; it's the equivalent of getting shoved in the chest. If anyone does that to me, I see red. You don't stop and go, "OK, just calm down." My family will ring me up and say, "Why don't you just smile and give them their shots and walk away? Why do you have to retaliate?" I'm like, "Because I want them to know that they can't just sit outside my house. I will throw an egg at them. This is my space, it's my house."' He admitted: 'I've thrown an egg – not at them, just kind of next to them so it splatters up against them, that's how pathetic it is, that's what we're reduced to. You can't actually stand up and slap them. When they kind of spy in on you and you're trying to like, bathe out in the sun, and you're with your girlfriend and your friends and your family... it actually feels like you're getting a slap across the face. And we can't physically stand up and hit them back, of course – it would be rude and against the law. So, you just get an egg...'

When he wasn't egg-throwing – most of the time – Heath's life was now progressing at an astonishingly rapid pace. As soon as he finished filming *Brokeback Mountain* he went to Venice to film *Casanova* and then returned to Australia to make a low-budget film, *Candy*, about a pair of young lovers in Melbourne, who also happen to be heroin addicts. It meant that there was practically a 'stockpile' of his films waiting for release in a short space of time, a number boosted by the delays on *The Brothers Grimm*, which meant that it would eventually be seen by the public at roughly the same time as his newer catalogue of work.

It was at the première of one of his films, the Los Angeles showing of *The Brothers Grimm*, that the news that had been bubbling under for months was finally publicly confirmed: Heath was to become a father. There had been unconfirmed reports as early as April that Michelle was attending pre-natal classes near the couple's Sydney home and when she stepped onto the red carpet in her first 'official' outing with Heath at the Directors Guild of America Theater in LA in August, her 'bump' was there for all to see, as was a sparkling diamond engagement ring.

The happiness that the couple felt was reflected in comment made by Heath at the time, though normally wary of any remarks about his private life, coming as it did at the end of a long period of filming 5 movies back-to-back: 'I want to spend at least a few months bonding. I might do something in the middle of next year because I'll have had a year off by then.'

Heath had already decided to move from Los Angeles to New York, where Michelle was based, and soon after that West Coast première he sold the Los Feliz home, where he had lived in for 5 years, for about double the price he paid for it. It sold for close to its $2.8 million – about £1.5 million – asking price. Hidden behind gates, it had a period courtyard, a fountain and vintage tiling throughout, but he had been on the road for most of the previous 5 years and had spent little time in the 1925-built Spanish-style home.

He also had other reasons for leaving: He told gay magazine *The Advocate*, 'If you were going to the f***ing 7-Eleven convenience store or going to drop your girl off at yoga or going to the dentist, anywhere, they [paparazzi] just follow you. There just happens to be, I guess, a bunch of celebrities that live in the Hollywood hills... and there are cars just everywhere, parked at the bottom of streets. And they know your car, so as soon as you go down there, they follow you. I don't want to raise my child in that environment. It was hard enough for Michelle to have to feel like she had to outrun these people; she would just turn her car around and not go to an appointment – or she wouldn't go visit a friend because she has cars following her; she would just come home and burst into tears.'

So home for the couple was now to be New York, where Michelle already lived and which was also nearer her family. At first the couple rented, but Heath's busy work schedule and the sale of the Los Angeles house meant he was able to spend $4.7 million (about £2.5 million) on his home in Boerum Hill, a small but affluent area in the north-western part of once run-down Brooklyn. He bought the 150-year-old house from Australian actress Nell Campbell, best known under her name 'Little Nell' for her role in *The Rocky Horror Show*. Campbell subsequently became a club owner in New York and the large house had been thoroughly refurbished by the time Heath and Michelle moved in to the corner brownstone building, with its high ceilings, a backyard garden and a deck on top of the garage. A mere 200 metres away the area became more grubby with graffiti and derelict buildings, but the couple's new home was undoubtedly in an up-and-coming part of the neighbourhood.

Heath loved the area – and the thought of soon being a father. In his own words, he and Michelle were 'experiencing just huge amounts of excitement' over the birth: 'I can't wait to meet my child. We've been preparing. We're both fit and happy and healthy – that's all you can ask for. I really appreciate Brooklyn because, quite frankly, no one gives a shit... The best thing about Brooklyn is it's removed. The paparazzi wouldn't even know how to get out to Carol Gardens [an area near his house], so I just live a really normal life. I lug my laundry down to the laundromat, I keep the house nice and tidy and clean, I go shopping at the supermarket and I cook. I commute on the train back and forth, in and out of town, and I sit and observe all these people around me, all these lives and these stories. It's really stimulating and I feel like I'm really living for the first time; it's wonderful.'

The couple, like any other first-time parents, were busy – in their case they had planned for a natural childbirth complete with a doula (a non-medical birthing guide who assists the mother) although they decided against hypno-birthing, with Heath saying, 'I don't think we'll be throwing Michelle into a trance.' They kept very early ultrasound pictures of the baby stuck to their fridge: 'There are two little nostril holes and then the shape of the lips – it's Michelle's mouth. It's so bizarre. These little porcelain lips that are exactly the same shape as Michelle's. It's just adorable,' the soon-to-be-father announced. 'I just need to meet her, I need to hold her.'

Heath was literally surrounded by women and reminders of them. As mentioned, across one wrist was tattooed the word 'KAOS' – which stands for Kate, Ashleigh, Olivia and Sally, his mother and three sisters. On the other arm was the phrase 'Old Man River', which Michelle had written there and he then had her handwriting tattooed over: 'There's something eternal about the phrase. Now I'm Old Man River. Life is about to speed up from this point on. It has nothing to do with show tunes, it's a little personal,' was all he would say. There was also a rope tattoo and the Canadian maple leaf on his right hand.

Michelle was by now referring to Heath as her 'husband' although they had no immediate plans for marriage, feeling that neither 'boyfriend' nor 'partner' was appropriate and, as the birth came near and nearer, she let slip that the child would be a girl. In Toronto to promote *Brokeback Mountain* she said, 'It's strange to watch the film now because it means so much more to me. I met my husband there, the seed of my daughter was born there – it's just really, really powerful. I had a few fantasies about a husband and a wedding when I was a little girl. But I'm really happy with things just the way they are right now.'

She was even happier on 28 October when their daughter was born in New York. Reports at the time were short on detail; it was far from a 'publicity-led' birth, and Heath expressed distaste for anything such as a photo-shoot for the child, but a few days later his father in Australia confirmed the good news: Kim Ledger said his son was thrilled by the arrival of the 2.83kg Matilda Rose. 'Heath is the cluckiest guy you'll ever meet. He's totally wrapped up in Matilda,' he said. Jake Gyllenhaal, godfather to Matilda, was able to say, tongue-in-cheek, 'Heath and I made love and they end up having a baby!'

The name was suitably Australian, but Michelle said it

was she who chose it: 'I came up with it on the subway one day. It just fell from the sky and into my head. And I love, love the Roald Dahl book *Matilda*. I didn't think about it at the time, but then afterwards, I was like, "Yeah, that's the girl I want: reads lots of books and makes things move with her eyes." That'll be my daughter, for sure.'

Neighbours were soon bringing the traditional lasagne round as a present for the couple, but work beckoned as Michelle still had to play her part in promoting *Brokeback Mountain*. She gave one interview less than two months after giving birth in which she admitted: 'I'm so tired. I feel ridiculous, all this hair and make-up. I just want to go home and go to bed and give her a bath.' The couple had managed to live in peace for some months in their house until a New York newspaper gave details of where they were living: 'We had lived in blissful anonymity. Then the story came out and there were photographers around the next day. I'm deeply shy and I don't like anybody looking at me.'

The couple didn't have a nanny, which meant they cared for Matilda themselves or, if they went out, with the help of Michelle's family. Heath's mother Sally and sister Kate also flew in to help. The happy parents, with baby Matilda, planned to spend Christmas with Michelle's family in Montana before heading for Australia: 'We really wanted to do everything ourselves, especially for this immediate time together,' said Michelle, who admitted her life had become 'a cycle of eating, washing, sleeping, cleaning... Now, for fun, I nap.' They were still wary of publicity, refusing to release pictures of the baby: 'When we go back to Australia, photographers are pretty relentless and it used to scare me and upset me. I have to try not to get too anxious, because anything I feel gets channelled straight to her,' the young mother said.

Although she was meant to talk of her part in the Ang Lee film, she had to admit that her main role at the time was: 'Matilda's mom – I love being a young parent. It's me, the baby and the breast pump. I'm getting very little sleep. But the difference between the day before I gave birth and the day after is like the old me and the new me. I knew having a baby would work some magic on me... I feel different in my body, and in my mind. And I don't think work will be like therapy anymore – my acting will be more about my characters and less about me.'

Heath noticed the strain on Michelle: 'Five weeks after you've had your baby, the mother shouldn't get out of her pyjamas, let alone get out of her house and into the spotlight and answering questions and taking photos. I mean, the poor thing is just completely exhausted... I am too, but men aren't allowed to complain because we're really hopeless and useless. We really do nothing in comparison to what the mothers have to go through. So I'm just doing everything I can at this point to give her, her sleep. I wake up early and look after the baby and let her sleep in until as long as she can.'

As he prepared for Christmas, Heath too was having to make some adjustments to his life to facilitate Matilda's arrival: 'Next year my hope is to spend as much time in

Australia as possible. I want to take Matilda back and introduce her to the ocean,' he said, although he was wary of photographers and their 'long lenses looking at your butt as you come out of the ocean.'

Like most young fathers he also admitted he had 'never felt so useless' as he was during the birth: 'Witnessing this innate, primal strength and determination that's injected into women when they have to push out that baby is just the most spectacular thing ever. I definitely walked away feeling that as men, over time we have over-compensated for our lack of strength and, witnessing this intimidating experience of women just being that much stronger than we are, we've gone out and created battles and wars and taken steroids and gone to the gym. So I happily relinquish power to her because, you know, I am not about to go out and create a war. Boy, do I love them both – and she's just a beautiful kid.'

The couple hadn't wed and he explained, 'I really don't feel like I need a piece of paper to validate the love I have for her. She's my soul mate and we couldn't love each other any more. My life right now is, I wouldn't say reduced to food, but my duties in life are that I wake up, I cook breakfast, clean the dishes, prepare lunch, clean those dishes, go to the market, get fresh produce, cook dinner, clean those dishes and then sleep, if I can. And I love it – I actually adore it. There's nothing work-wise on the horizon yet, but I will have to go back to work some time next year to pay off my house!'

Living in his new leafy neighbourhood was also a thrill

for Heath: 'Moving to Brooklyn is the greatest decision we ever made. We really blend in there. We're friends with all our neighbours, and they come around with lasagnes, and we go to community dinners and we're carolling for the holidays. Fatherhood is what I've always wanted. It definitely exceeds my expectations, and I was always expecting a lot.'

His running dispute with some of the Australian press continued when the couple flew to Australia for the première of *Brokeback Mountain* early in 2006. He even telephoned the *Daily Telegraph* there to protest innocence over allegations that both he and his uncle had spat at the media. He admitted that in the past he had been 'out of line' but said, 'It's disgusting and awful – I would never in a million years do anything like that; I'm not some sort of dirty spitter. I'm trying to get by back here and live a nice polite life with my family. I'm learning to deal with it a bit better, I think I am.'

His egg-throwing, verbal abuse and finger gestures were a thing of the past he said, adding, 'I can admit it's a little out of line to pull the finger out and I'm trying not to do that anymore. I'm trying to bite my finger these days.'

He was also in a consolatory mood when he spoke to the *Sun-Herald* newspaper on the same visit, explaining his newly found peace of mind brought about by Michelle and Matilda: 'It's a trip. It's incredible to what level the film has changed my life. I mean, it's given me an incredible amount of synchronicity. I have these two girls that I fall deeper and deeper in love with daily and that is, hands down, the greatest gift that I've been given from this. I'll forever be grateful.

'I think you have a certain level of responsibility to "man-up" so to speak. Fatherhood or parenthood is ultimately the most selfless act you can participate in, so in order to be so selfless you have to be healthy-minded and healthy-spirited in order to focus in wholly on this other person and making them happy and safer. So you're forced into ironing out any kinks. That's certainly the way I'm approaching parenthood. I'm not sure if it's the right way, it's just my way.'

He added: 'I'm feeling the need to explain myself clearly these days as opposed to the past when I was more protective and deflective and defensive about my private life... because that just gave everyone else the opportunity to fabricate their own answers to who I am and what my life is. Now I've brought this very special child into my life and I have this very special girl in my life, I don't want them to be misrepresented or my love for them to be misrepresented either. I'd rather explain the way it really is than let other people guess... So you just learn to deal with it, relax with it, be more diplomatic about it and then hopefully it will relieve you of that stress. Which it has, because I care less about it now and care more about just being happy with my own family.'

Michelle was diplomatic too at the première of their film in rainy Melbourne, where over 1,000 fans gathered to see the couple walk hand-in-hand down the red carpet: 'Now Australia is my second home and we want to spend equal time in both places. It's nice to get to know both Melbourne and Sydney.'

It was nevertheless taxing for her so soon after giving birth and she confessed to *Interview* magazine: 'It's been hectic since she was about a month old. It seems like nearly every day there's been something that didn't involve just the three of us, something extracurricular to deal with. But through it all, from every morning when we all wake up together to every night when we all go to bed together, I feel I've only been getting closer to him and to her. I don't feel like any of it has taken me truly away. It's been such a learning curve to work and to be a mother. My mom didn't do that, so I don't have a reference for it. It's certainly a worthwhile balance, but I started off with too much ambition doing all this press. I thought that my body had healed from the delivery, so I made the mistake of saying yes to doing all these things and ended up feeling so anguished to be away from her – and crying as a result. Your body tells you all this. You know, the milk's coming down, your mind's not your own anymore – or your vocabulary or your memory. It's all because you're thinking about one thing, the welfare of your child. So I get constant reminders. Now we kind of have a little system going, a little understanding of what we all need.'

The première of *Brokeback Mountain* was marred, however, when a small group of photographers sprayed Heath with a water pistol as a 'joke' in what they said was a response to his past behaviour towards them. But it had a deeper effect on him than anyone realised at the time. He later said: 'That broke my heart. They obviously wanted me to punch and swear at them, looking a big bad idiot, but I was crushed. I had to introduce the film, but I could barely speak. I went straight home to Bronte, got into the bathroom and broke down.'

The next morning he wanted to surf outside his home but found he was under siege from TV crews, reporters and photographers: 'They kept ringing my doorbell, demanding I come out. One paparazzi was on my front step, with his daughter, holding a big bunch of roses and giving TV interviews, saying he wanted to apologise to Michelle, but that they had to teach me a lesson, I needed to be brought down a peg...

'We were like prisoners in our own house, our own goldfish bowl, it turned out. I'd installed dark reflective glass on the balconies and windows, but they had special lenses to shoot pictures of us through the glass. I felt so stressed and disheartened. I wanted Michelle to love Australia, but we couldn't live like that. It never let up, so after 10 days we packed our bags, flew to America and I put the house on the market.' He added, 'Some paparazzi chant at me, "Can't you take it, Heath? You shouldn't be in showbiz if you can't take being followed and photographed. You need us, Heath!" No, I freakin' don't!'

Soon afterwards it was revealed that he had indeed decided to put his home on the market for almost £3 million. The house where he had had to establish a base was sadly just not suitable for such a high-profile couple. Heath had lovingly furnished it with a 'shabby-chic' sofa, smart leather chairs, two chess sets, three barbecues and polished concrete work surfaces. The walls were white and the colour broken up by dark timber supports. The house was also home to his collection of CDs: Macy Gray, Bob Dylan REM, U2, David Bowie and Janis Joplin mingled with recordings of Mozart and other classical composers. The below-ground theatre-room, reached by wide wooden steps held up with wrought-iron balustrades, had a rich chocolate carpet and a 3.5 metre-wide framed viewing screen.

Although it was in a beautiful beachside position, its large glass windows meant that privacy was at a premium. Heath had solved the problem by having the glass tinted around the balcony, but this still meant that he and his family were very much in view to passers-by and photographers if they used the terraces. He put it bluntly to his local paper in Perth, who he telephoned one day from Los Angeles. During the conversation he described the difficulties he'd faced with the state-of-the art house: 'My home in Bronte, you know, is a fishbowl and I can't see a future there, unfortunately. My Dad found the house and I bought it pretty much off the Internet and once I got there I found it's situated in a really unfortunate position where people can look up into it.'

His hopes of being able to live in Australia with his family were dashed – home from now on would be Brooklyn.

CHAPTER 13

THE 'NEW BRANDO'

It was 5.30a.m. on 31 January 2006 when the telephone rang in Heath and Michelle's hotel room in Los Angeles. Nearby little Matilda was finally asleep, as were her parents. The baby had woken them three times during the evening: at midnight, 3a.m. and then 5a.m. and now the entire family were slumbering, desperately trying to catch up on their sleep.

On the line was a member of Heath's publicity team, excitedly telling him the wonderful, early-morning news: 'You've been nominated for an Oscar.' He turned to Michelle and passed on the information; he also gave her more good news – she too had been nominated, in the 'Best Supporting Actress' role. Then he kissed her – and they both went back to sleep!

It was understandable. They were exhausted and had reached the stage all parents kept awake by a small child throughout the night eventually arrive at, all they cared about was sleep.

No one would suggest that Heath would have been at all blasé about the nomination, but if he had been then it might have been understandable: *Brokeback Mountain* had become one of the most acclaimed films in recent cinematic history. Ang Lee's direction, the script, the performances of the stars, all had been showered in praise and awards and nowhere was that applause louder than it was for his performance.

The buzz about the film was already gathering even during the time it was being made and that murmur grew louder once filming had finished. By the time Heath had flown into Venice in early September 2005 for its famous Film Festival, the noise had reached a crescendo.

Venice is the oldest film festival in the world, dating back to 1932, and its première award is The Golden Lion – the Leone d'Oro – and *Brokeback Mountain* was one of the contenders to win the prize. Other stars jetting in apart from Heath included Russell Crowe, George Clooney, Matt Damon and Gwyneth Paltrow. Like him they too had films to promote, although they didn't have the problem he faced.

They all had one film each to push – Heath had three!

Brokeback Mountain alone should have been a source of pride to Heath, an actor who by his own admission, 'had taken the shine off my career,' only a short time before. But *Brokeback* wasn't the only film of his showing; alongside it was the much-delayed *The Brothers*

Grimm, like *Brokeback* an entry for the Golden Lion award, and his recently filmed *Casanova*, in which he played the title role of the legendary seducer, was also being premièred at the Festival.

The normally staid *Daily Telegraph* of London remarked, 'The thought occurs that this year's Venice should be renamed "The Heath Ledger Festival." The 26-year-old Australian actor stars in three high-profile films here, all of them screened in the past three days. His face (blond, tousled hair, narrow gaze, tight lips) scowls from a dozen billboards; his large footprints are leaving deep impressions on the red carpet at the Sala Grande's premières.'

The 'neutral' Agence France Press news agency too was moved to note: 'Move aside, George Clooney. Australia's answer to "Gorgeous George," young Heath Ledger, is fast taking over the Venice Film Festival, fronting three new movies premièring here and eclipsing the former festival darling. Clooney's film opened the official competition for the Golden Lion with *Good Night, and Good Luck*. Many here believe he may well be back to claim the award for Best Film when the event winds up next weekend, but meanwhile the mantle of festival seducer has passed to Ledger. When Italy's leading daily *Corriere della Sera* repeatedly referred to the 28-year-old as "Heat Ledger" in one of its Venice reviews last week, it may not have been unintentional, so commercially hot has he become.'

And so it went on. Heath was inevitably the talk of the Festival. He tried to play it down by saying he was in a 'slight state of denial', adding: 'I get nervous when I have to talk about movies. So I'm pretending I have just one in the festival. It's an honour and it's exciting but I'm exhausted from promoting each one,' although he was moved to announce, 'It's the most exciting time of my life.' At such a high time in both his work and private life – Michelle was due to give birth just two months after the Festival – he also had his feet firmly on the ground. Speaking about why he had chosen to do so many films in such a short space of time, he said: 'I'd finally destroyed it [his career] and I had to rebuild it and that's why I went off and did five films back-to-back, because I was like, "It's time to mend this open wound." I got to work with really wonderful directors and wonderful people and it's been the most exciting year of my career. I wanted to look at all five projects as one, like it was a boxed set of what I could do, or what I want to be able to do.'

Italy seemed to have fallen in love with Heath, and the feeling appeared to be reciprocated. Heath, perhaps with his thoughts on his unborn child – he had already pronounced that 'Hollywood is no place to bring up a kid' – even dropped a hint that he might stay in the country. 'I have kind of been living out of bags for the past 13 years. I will just stick to that. Home is, like, Earth. I don't care where I land. I am actually thinking of going to live in Italy. The food and the wine are great. That's it really. Oh, we have a couple of plans; we have a few places up our sleeves. I would much rather work in Europe than America.'

His affection for all things Italian would have increased

at the end of the Venice Film Festival when *Brokeback Mountain* won the Golden Lion prize. The triumph can hardly have caused a sensation as it had been so well received by both the critics and audiences alike. It nevertheless caused Ang Lee to change his plans, having to leave the Toronto Film Festival (which was opening) to cross the Atlantic and collect his prize. As he accepted his award, he referred to the film as a 'great American love story' that is 'unique and so universal... I'm so glad it's prevailed here and was received so warmly here.'

It was 'warmly' received elsewhere too. Critics, judging panels and, importantly, audiences loved the film. A brief selection of the reviews it received as it opened around the world sums up the feeling of the men and women who often dissected films without mercy but were smitten by the film and Heath's performance.

When the film opened in America the praise it received seemed endless. Leading the way was the *New York Times*, who said: 'The lonesome chill that seeps through Ang Lee's epic western, *Brokeback Mountain*, is as bone deep as the movie's heartbreaking story of two cowboys who fall in love almost by accident. It is embedded in the craggy landscape where their idyll begins and ends. It creeps into the farthest corners of the wide-open spaces they share with coyotes, bears and herds of sheep and rises like a stifled cry into the big, empty sky that stretches beyond the horizon. Both Mr. Ledger and Mr. Gyllenhaal make this anguished love story physically palpable. Mr. Ledger magically and mysteriously disappears beneath the skin of his lean, sinewy character. It is a great screen performance, as good as the best of Marlon Brando and Sean Penn. The pain and disappointment felt by Jack, who is softer, more self-aware and self-accepting, continually registers in Mr. Gyllenhaal's sad, expectant silver-dollar eyes.'

Another highly respected US film critic, Peter Travers, wrote: 'Ledger's magnificent performance is an acting miracle. He seems to tear it from his insides. Ledger doesn't just know how Ennis moves, speaks and listens; he knows how he breathes. To see him inhale the scent of a shirt hanging in Jack's closet is to take measure of the pain of love lost.'

Kenneth Turan in the *Los Angeles Times* was equally enthusiastic: '*Brokeback Mountain* is a groundbreaking film because it isn't. It's a deeply felt, emotional love story that deals with the uncharted, mysterious ways of the human heart just as so many mainstream films have before it. The two lovers here just happen to be men. Big star vehicles with homosexual protagonists are, of course, not new; one of them, 1993's *Philadelphia*, even won a Best Actor Oscar for star Tom Hanks. But these films invariably have had an air of earnest special pleading about them, a sense that they'd rather do good in the world than tell a good story. Instead of emphasising its apartness, *Brokeback Mountain* insists it is a romance like any other, and that makes all the difference.

'Confidently directed by Ang Lee and featuring sensitive and powerful performances by Jake Gyllenhaal and a breathtaking Heath Ledger, this film is determined to involve us in the naturalness and even inevitability of its epic, complicated love story... *Brokeback Mountain* would not be the success it is without excellent acting across the board. Though he is hampered by an unconvincing ageing job, Gyllenhaal brings a fine harum-scarum energy and feeling to Jack's character, and Williams, glummer than she ever was in *The Station Agent*, illuminates all the corners of Alma's sadness. But, more than any of the others, Ledger brings this film alive by going so deeply into his character you wonder if he'll be able to come back. Aside from his small but strong part in *Monster's Ball*, nothing in the Australian-born Ledger's previous credits prepares us for the power and authenticity of his work here as a laconic, interior man of the West, a performance so persuasive that *Brokeback Mountain* could not have succeeded without it. Ennis' pain, his rage, his sense of longing and loss are real for the actor, and that makes them unforgettable for everyone else.'

The *Wall Street Journal*'s verdict was: 'The triumph is that of Heath Ledger, a young Australian who has been known until now as a hunky heart-throb. He's certainly handsome enough here, but in a touchingly bleak self-contained way. He doesn't portray his powerful, sometimes rugged cowboy so much as release him – slowly, quietly, tactfully, economically even reluctantly or so it would seem, until he has outed Ennis's lyrical soul.'

The *Daily Telegraph* in London, along with the rest of the British press, was equally enthusiastic: 'At its heart are performances by two actors – Jake Gyllenhaal and, even more notably, Heath Ledger – who seem to have been content to wallow in their status as easy-on-the-eye Hollywood young Turks. By agreeing to star in this film, both set themselves – and have triumphantly overcome – a huge challenge. That challenge has nothing to do with stripping off and clambering all over each other; man-to-man smooching is no big deal in today's metro-sexual media climate. Rather, it's to take on parts infinitely more complex and subtle than those they or their generation of actors are used to... Ledger is an utter revelation. He reins in the hard-bodied physicality that he has brandished in most of his films. He's the more fearful of the two men, a poorly-educated hick who believes in actions rather than words. He speaks with a gravelly murmur, as if he's already six feet under the earth.'

Back home in Australia the reception was just as warm. Heath had not always enjoyed the best of relationships with some of the country's media, even having to apologise for eating an orange during one televised interview, but that in no way seemed to diminish their praise for his acting in the epic. Two reviews give a brief taste of the reception the film received.

The *West Australian* said: 'The film's great strength is the deft, delicate direction of Ang Lee, who not just cements the bond between his stars but weds them closely to the harshly beautiful landscape. The film has a primal, almost mythical quality (as do all the great Westerns, which this film alludes to despite Lee's denial he's making a Western).

But, most importantly, it is the utterly convincing, deeply moving performances of Ledger and Gyllenhaal, whose characters' inability to break though the barriers and live as man and man (it's also a wrenching study of masculine inarticulateness and dysfunctionality) will have even the toughest *hombres* reaching for their girlfriend's handkerchiefs. Even though Gyllenhaal's swoon-inducing looks are amusingly at odds with the character in the original story, who is described by Proulx as short, fat and buck-toothed, he has just the right measure of sexy masculine swagger to turn the heads of cowboy and cowgirl alike. But it's the breathtaking turn by Ledger as a man whose inability to face his true nature has left him a knot of anger and anguish, a man for whom even the simplest utterance reveals too much of his shredded soul, for which *Brokeback Mountain* will be chiefly remembered. Ledger might not quite be the equal of Marlon Brando, as the *New York Times* famously suggested. But if the Perth-born Oscar contender keeps channelling his pain in the way he does so bravely, so artfully in *Brokeback Mountain*, greatness is certainly on the horizon.'

The *Age* newspaper agreed, adding: 'The two actors both illuminate and inhabit their characters: they are compelling but low-key interpretations. Gyllenhaal, wide-eyed and pretty, has the lighter, more extroverted role, while Ledger gives an exceptional, devastating depiction of a man living a life of quiet desperation, a character folding in on himself, winding his emotions and his world in tighter and tighter.'

And so it went on. The film was loved by critics and audiences alike. The original fears that its theme would alienate many film-goers proved ill-founded. James Schamus, producer of the film, was adamant, however, that it was never targeted at a gay audience, although it was assumed men would go along if they did 'not want to look like a complete troglodyte to their girlfriends.'

The original target audience was women. 'The audience is literally anybody who likes a true, epic love story. And clearly, that starts with women. Of course, we have a core audience of art-film and gay and lesbian film-goers, who I think will seek it out. But this film appeals to female viewers almost without exception – which is a wonderful place to be, obviously, because women drive the art-house film business.' He added: 'This is a film that we've now seen has resonance for people from every persuasion, walk of life and background. I think the audience is straight, gay, male, female.' It was marketed as a romance, the famous poster of Heath in profile and Jake behind him deliberately chosen to emphasise that mood.

In America the film did good business in the 'sophisticated cities' of New York, Los Angeles and San Francisco, which perhaps was not too surprising But it also drew the audiences in Middle America, where some had feared its subject matter might not appeal so much. That proved to be far from the case, with audience figures actually growing as word-of-mouth added to the practically unanimous praise from the critics.

When it opened just before Christmas 2005 in selected

cinemas across America, the movie faced fierce box-office competition. Two blockbusters, *King Kong*, starring Naomi Watts, and *The Chronicles of Narnia* opened at the same time and were showing at a vastly greater number of cinemas, thereby bringing in higher revenue. But an interesting statistic emerged: over the holiday period *Brokeback* earned $13,599 per theatre it showed at compared with $9,305 for *King Kong* and $8,225 for *The Chronicles of Narnia: The Lion, the Witch and the Wardrobe*.

A handful of cinemas banned the film, prompting Heath to state that West Virginia was a state 'that was lynching people only 25 years ago' but the vast majority of the country took the movie to its heart. The momentum continued as it was shown at an increasing number of theatres and was then given a boost with the announcement of 8 nominations for the forthcoming Oscars.

It is worth noting the full list as an aid to assessing the impact the film had. In addition to Heath's Best Actor bid there were: Best Picture, Best Supporting Actor (Jake Gyllenhaal), Best Supporting Actress (Michelle Williams), Best Director (Ang Lee), Best Adapted Screenplay (Larry McMurtry and Diana Ossana), Best Cinematography and Best Original Score (Gustavo Santaolalla). It was a staggering achievement and fully reflected the esteem in which the picture was held.

It would have been appropriate, therefore, if the film had swept the boards on 5 March, but it was not to be. Ang Lee won Best Director and the screenwriters and composer

Santaolalla also won their categories. Heath did not pick up the Best Actor award – he would have been the youngest-ever winner had he done so – instead that went to Philip Seymour Hoffman for his portrayal of writer Truman Capote. Best Film belonged to *Crash*, the controversial story of race relations in Los Angeles.

Ang Lee summed up many people's feelings over Heath's failure to win the Oscar: 'I think his performance is outstanding and in film history, it will be something that will be remembered. It's not only remarkable but a miracle. A lot of people told me he reminds them of a young Brando.' Later that evening Heath and Michelle arrived at the post-Oscar party held by *Vanity Fair* at West Hollywood's Morton's restaurant. The bash is legendary and it is said to be harder to get into it than it is to get into the Awards ceremony itself. They decided to go in quickly rather than talk to photographers outside, some of whom booed and jeered him when they realised he wasn't going to stop. He cheekily responded with a two-finger gesture over his shoulder before they began to mingle with Nicole Kidman, Keith Urban, Naomi Watts, Mick Jagger, Lindsay Lohan, Madonna, Philip Seymour Hoffman, Joaquin Phoenix, Reese Witherspoon and Robert Altman, among others.

For a film of such importance it was surprising that it failed to sweep the board, a fact highlighted by Annie Proulx's rather scathing piece about both the ceremony and the winners and losers, written some days later in the *Guardian* newspaper. She didn't pull her punches and wrote: 'None of the acting awards came *Brokeback*'s way, you betcha. The prize, as expected, went to Philip Seymour Hoffman for his brilliant portrayal of Capote, but in the months preceding the awards thing, there has been little discussion of acting styles and various approaches to character development by this year's nominees. Hollywood loves mimicry, the conversion of a film actor into the spittin' image of a once-living celeb. But which takes more skill, acting a person who strolled the boulevard a few decades ago and who left behind tapes, film, photographs, voice recordings and friends with strong memories, or the construction of characters from imagination and a few cold words on the page? I don't know. The subject never comes up. Cheers to David Strathairn, Joaquin Phoenix and Hoffman, but what about actors who start in the dark?'

It was a clear reference to Heath and his colleagues, but there was more from her pen about her night at the Oscars: 'The hours sped by on wings of boiler plate. *Brokeback*'s first award was to Argentinean Gustavo Santaolalla for the film's plangent and evocative score. Later came the expected award for screenplay adaptation to Diana Ossana and Larry McMurtry, and only a short time later the Director's Award to Ang Lee. And that was it, three awards, putting it on equal footing with *King Kong*. When Jack Nicholson said best picture went to *Crash*, there was a gasp of shock, and then applause from many – the choice was a hit with the home team since the film is set in Los Angeles. It was a safe pick of "controversial film" for the heffalumps.'

She finished off the article thus: 'For those who call this little piece a Sour Grapes Rant, play it as it lays.' If the final tally of awards from the Oscars was a little surprising in that it failed to reflect the impact of the film, there was consolation elsewhere, however. For there were other awards to be collected, including a clutch of BAFTAs and Golden Globes. The film was unstoppable. It ended up as the fifth highest earning Western of all time and the eighth highest romance. At the American box offices, it earned over $80 million and $95 million throughout the rest of the world – staggering figures for a film made on such a modest budget.

There had never been a movie like it, before – or since. All those connected with it, from the writers and Ang Lee through to all the actors deserved the praise that was heaped on them, but one man stood out above them all. It was undoubtedly Heath Ledger's finest hour and one that will be relived every time the film is watched in the years to come.

CHAPTER 14

THE JOYS OF FATHERHOOD

Brokeback Mountain may have been the film that made Heath Ledger a 'superstar', but the filming had taken its toll on him. Once his commitments to the soon-to-be classic had finished, he needed a change of scenery and lifestyle and this was to come in the shape of the title role in a film of a completely different nature, *Casanova*.

He exchanged the isolation of the Canadian Rockies for the elegance and history of Venice to film a new version of the story of Giovanni Giacomo Casanova, the 18th-century adventurer and author whose name has become synonymous with womanising. A friend of Mozart and Voltaire, it was the romantic aspect of his life that made him famous even 200 years after his death and has prompted several writers and directors to try and capture his story on film.

This time the man trying for a fresh take on the Venetian

was Lasse Hallstrom, the Swedish director behind *What's Eating Gilbert Grape*, *The Cider House Rules* and *Chocolat*. Coincidentally he had also directed *The Shipping News*, the film adaptation of the novel by E. Annie Proulx, the writer of *Brokeback*. This would be a completely different tone from the cowboy epic, however. It was to be played very much for laughs and alongside Heath would be Jeremy Irons and Sienna Miller.

Heath didn't try and come up with an extravagant reasons for taking the role: '*Brokeback Mountain* was such an excruciating shoot, pretty horrendous at times. This was like a working holiday by comparison. Since my profession had wound me up, I needed something in my profession to wind me down – I couldn't just go home; I would have gone mad. So I went to Venice, floated around the city, drank wine, ate pasta. I needed to just breathe, relax... and got paid for it. I had a super time making that. It was six months in Venice, so it was just beautiful. And I got picked up in a boat every morning. It was just magic and it was fun. We didn't take it seriously whatsoever – it's Tom Stoppardish, certainly not Fellini's version of *Casanova*. It was basically a working holiday, an elaborate extended period of unwinding, so I could unravel myself from *Brokeback Mountain*.

'It was really fun, just working in Venice. The city should only exist in your dreams. Getting picked up every morning in a boat. There are no camera trucks; there are camera boats. There are no trailers to hang out in. There are the streets and chairs. It's all very communal. All the cast would sit around and play dice games. I wanted something I could bang out, something I didn't have to take too seriously, and essentially this was it because we were borrowing Casanova's name to have a little fun. So I ate and drank and passed out every night and got picked up by a boat every morning to go to the set. I went straight from *Brokeback* to Venice, so it was pretty much a working environment. It was such a wonderful environment that Lasse had created for us. It was amazing working in Venice; it was like shooting a film inside a museum. We were lucky in that usually films will shoot the exteriors and then bugger off to Luxembourg or London or somewhere, but we had permission to shoot interiors, so we had a great time.'

No one could accuse him of immersing himself in the history of Casanova; he cheerfully admitted knowing little about the man: 'I knew the obvious points, and going into the film I read up on him and flicked through his journals. But once we read the script and sat around discussing the direction we wanted to take the film, we threw that out the window. We wanted to be free of any restraint or responsibility to represent the historical Casanova. He's certainly an interesting man, a lot more interesting than the character I'm playing in the movie. I mean, my version is a completely sugar-coated version of the real man. I don't do any justice to him whatsoever and I certainly wasn't trying to. We're making what Lasse calls a romp and we wanted a clean slate so that we could have fun and enjoy ourselves.'

Even this cleaned-up Disney production managed to create controversy with its R rating, despite every effort to play down the story's eroticism. The 'Restricted' rating meant that in the United States no one under the age of 17 could see it without being accompanied by an adult. The decision annoyed the director as well Heath's co-star Sienna Miller. 'I think it's unfortunate that the movie's gotten an R rating,' Heath said. 'Had we known it was going to get an R, we would have made it a little closer to deserving it. We would've pumped up the sexual content and gone to town. As it is, I don't see anything R-rated in it whatsoever. There's no sex, there's no profanity. It's pathetic, really.'

The light-hearted effect the director was seeking permeated the film set. Heath jokingly called Sienna Miller 'big bum' after one sequence in which she wore a corset and he split his tight trousers during a fencing scene. She fired back, 'He split his trousers on a lunge, which made me laugh and that broke the ice from Day One.'

It was a role that Heath obviously enjoyed playing, both for its humour and the opportunity of enjoying one of the most beautiful cities on earth. He was to receive good reviews for his performance too when the film was released as one of his 'back-to-back' movies although he later felt he had 'missed the boat' in his performance. It was a common feeling to his own performances; often he felt afterwards that he could have done better.

Nor was he always satisfied with some of the work he was offered and would, at times, accept. On occasions he would even phone his agent to try and get out of a role: 'He knows it's a routine, I know it's a routine. It feels like it's necessary to put myself down. It inspires me to focus more and work harder. I don't really like to do the same thing twice. I like to do something I fear. I like to set up obstacles and defeat them. I like to be afraid of the project. I always am. When I get cast in something, I always believe I shouldn't have been cast. There's a huge amount of anxiety that drowns out any excitement I have toward the project. Pretty much any time I've signed on to a movie, I've tried to get out of it.'

When he did get home, he was revelling in his role as what one observer called, 'Brooklyn's most famous father': 'I'm Mr. Mom. Every day I wake up and prepare two breakfasts: I get Michelle granola and cook her an egg, I clean the dishes, and then I'm cooking lunch. Later, I go out to the market and get fresh produce for dinner, and then I cook that. And I love it! I love my new job.

'When I'm not working, I like to really de-attach myself. I don't want to be tempted, either. In my personal life, however, I want to achieve more babies! For the first time I feel I am a part of life. It feels like you commit to life. There is something cosmic about it, like you feel more connected to the universe, as opposed to before when you just felt like you were floating around as a ghost. I'm now participating in life. Matilda's such an awesome, beautiful little girl that Michelle and I hate spending five minutes away from her, never mind five months, so it has to be really, really worth it. I adore where I live. I love the real sense of community: I love my neighbours, I love the coffee shop down the road. We really are left there to live. It feels like we're on an island when we're just next to one.'

If *Casanova* had been a fairly light-hearted film, both in the final movie and as a work experience, the same could not be said for Heath's next venture, a harrowing film about a pair of young lovers who happened to be heroin addicts. *Candy* gave him the first chance in years to work in Australia and a welcome break in that he didn't have to use an accent either: 'I'm constantly looking for material in Australia because I thoroughly enjoy being free of the restraints of accents,' he said. 'It's a novel thing for me too. It's been 8 years since I've used my own accent. When you're doing an accent, if you have to laugh, nine times out of ten you'll laugh and you'll lose your accent.'

It also gave him the opportunity to deliver another outstanding performance as poet Dan, whose life spirals downwards as he struggles unsuccessfully to cope with his addiction. He drags young artist Candy, a fine portrayal by Abbie Cornish, down with him, pushing her into prostitution, in a harrowing film that pulls no punches, either in language or its depiction of the drug-taker's lifestyle.

Based on the story of one-time drug addict Luke Davies, who wrote the script, Heath's performance was rated by some as every bit as formidable as *Brokeback Mountain*. Sadly it failed to achieve the wider applause of *Brokeback* simply because the film didn't have the same international impact.

During filming Heath talked about how he faced the challenge of filming the role – and at one stage even injected himself to explore the mind-set of a drug addict! This was how he described setting about it: 'I had no desperate secret desire to play a junkie, it was just something I haven't done. Physically I stayed out of the sun and I tried to eat less but for all the technical aspects of it, Abby and I went to this centre in Sydney called NUAOA, which is the Narcotics Users Association Of Australia. We met a gentleman who has been using, and still is, I think, over the past 20 years and he took us into a boardroom and he opened up what looked like a rifle case and inside was a prosthetic arm, which was designed to train nurses.

'Within this centre it was designed to train young drug addicts how to find a vein and it was a fully functional kind of thing. Inside, the veins are fully functional and the two tubes that you can attach, like veins, have blood bags. We pumped blood through the arm and you could find a vein and then we find a vein and the nurse showed us how to do that, and you could even pump blood out of the arm and put the drugs through and then he showed us how to tie the tourniquets. And then the rest, like the drying-out sequence, we just had someone on set who could take us through the stages step by step from experience. Now you're in a cold sweat and in this next scene your stomach feels like it's just twisting up into a knot, your headaches, you're botched, they just kind of spelt it out for us... And we just responded to his knowledge of it.'

One questioner wanted to know what he thought of

celebrities who used drugs. Heath replied, 'It's obvious that it's not just celebrities in rehab, it's probably a similar statistic to just people outside of the industry but I do think that drugs and alcohol have been glorified and exoticised in such a way that it gets into the art world. Whether it's just watching the way that Jackson Pollock paints with a bottle of booze in his hand and a cigarette hanging out of his mouth, we've kind of connected that to what it takes to create something. When in fact it's anything but the truth. I mean, obviously creation comes out of the mind and it's hard to create when you're in that state. But I'm sure drugs and alcohol perhaps would inspire new thoughts and it's certainly not something that I use as a tool or a mechanism to create.'

But he didn't think the film would glamorise drug-taking: 'I can't honestly say that it was a concern of mine. I guess because I knew the context within the script, I knew it wasn't really glorifying it. I felt, I was hoping… So I think it ended up being a bit of a cautionary tale above anything. I feel like nearly everyone knows how to play a junkie by now. As a subject, it's been really over-exposed. You see it in movies, on TV and in books and magazines. We all know that it's going to be painful.'

The love story centres on how Candy is lured into his way of life: 'I guess it's a love triangle between them and the drug. I think they're just kind of intertwined. But I think we were all telling ourselves that it was more a love story than a story of heroin. The scripts in Australia are slim pickings these days and it was the best one available.' Tellingly, he said, 'I do think that drugs and alcohol have been glorified in the art world and what it takes to create. But creation comes from your mind and it's hard to create when you're fazed and drugged out. I'm sure drugs and alcohol would perhaps inspire new thoughts but it's certainly not something I use as a tool to create.'

Anyone who saw his subsequent masterly performance would find his remark about how detached he could be from the role extremely surprising: 'It doesn't really affect me personally. I kind of save that living through it part for that moment between "Action!" and "Cut!" and certainly when the film's over I just throw it all away and I'm very excited to get back home.'

Director Neil Armfield, highly regarded for his theatre work, wanted to rehearse scenes to perfection before a take but Heath explained, 'Abbie and I don't want to capture our performance in rehearsal. We're superstitious and nervous about it because we're not sure we can repeat it in the shoot. But Neil backed down and let us work in our own patterns.' That even included the young couple disappearing to a pub for a few drinks before some of their 'high' scenes. It worked perfectly.

After filming was completed the director admitted, 'I often thought Heath was under-acting. I couldn't see with my naked eye what he was doing, but on the big screen, he was right, perfect. And I often thought he was speaking too softly, but again, he was right. He also wanted to cut a lot of the dialogue out. I insisted on filming it anyway, then I have to say he was 90 per cent right there too, because I cut the dialogue in the edit.'

Heath's search for perfection even led him to one amazing take where he actually injected himself: 'I did one scene they didn't end up using. It was near the end of the movie when I inject again after being clean. There was a shot that we had, a tight shot of my arm, and I slipped the needle in and pulled back until you saw the blood, and then they went off it onto my face. I actually injected. It had water, colour and sugar in it to make it look watery brown. And then we found out that was the difference between a Mature rating and an R: the penetration. When it looked like it was going in and it didn't really go in, that was OK.'

He was more than prepared to admit, 'I've smoked pot before, and I know what it feels like to be high. But I've never been addicted to anything other than cigarettes, although that's quite a f***in' addiction. Also the subject of heroin... there's so many television documentaries and shows and movies and books, you kind of feel you know how they do it, even if you've never been anywhere near it.' Asked if drugs ever held a fascination for him he replied, again honestly, 'Mildly, as a teenager, but never to this extent. I was lucky that I never got pulled into any of those alleys.'

It's hard to imagine a more graphic scene than the one in which Heath injected himself, even if it did not make it to the film's final cut. But *Candy* contained an even more harrowing moment: Candy, played by Cornish, miscarries in agony and Heath is shocked to discover her loss, vividly shown on-screen. He played it in the knowledge that

Michelle was just beginning her pregnancy with his child: 'It was really terrible shooting that. We found out just a month earlier that we were having a baby. I don't usually get disturbed by scenes, no matter how dark they are, but that was really tough. In between takes, I was running off and calling Michelle, telling her I loved her. I didn't want to jinx my personal life with this scene. I actually protested about it a lot; I didn't want to look at the baby, and I didn't want Neil to shoot it at all. I would have liked it to be more suggested than graphic, but you do actually see a lot less on film than was shot, which I'm glad about. But it was still pretty horrible, this little prosthetic baby, all bloody, which looked so real. It wasn't nice.'

After *Candy* was wrapped up, Heath was to begin a fairly long period of 'paternity leave' to make up for all the filming and promotion work that had eaten into his precious family time. He and Michelle bought what he termed a 'one-bedroomed tree-house' in Los Angeles for when they were in the city. He was underplaying the elegance of the home somewhat. Although it was called 'The Treehouse', the Hollywood Hills house, not too far from his old home, cost $2.3 million and was in a sycamore grove on a half-acre lot and boasted a large teak deck. The post-and-beam house, built in 1951, was renovated in 2004, when it was owned by talk-show host Ellen DeGeneres, who lived on the property with her Australian partner, actress Portia de Rossi.

'When Michelle is working, I'm the nanny, and when I'm working, Michelle's the nanny. And so when she was working in LA, I was in a hotel room and it was really hard. Whether we like it or not, we go in and out of LA all the time,' was the reason Heath gave for the purchase.

The couple tried to enjoy time together although the paparazzi were still a nuisance, albeit not quite as bad as they had been previously. There was, however, a photographer who followed them around Brooklyn one day and Heath, in his own words, 'slaughtered him with kindness.' He, Michelle and Matilda were in a flower store when they spotted him and Heath said he grabbed a flower, ran out in the street and gave the camera-man the flower and said, 'If I give you this flower please, please, please do not take a photo of our daughter.'

'He didn't want to take it but eventually he took the flower and put his camera away and jumped in his car and left us, which was really nice of him. We probably get two lone photographers who wander out to Brooklyn maybe twice a year. It's the closest we've ever come to feeling like we can lead a normal life, so we really value it. We know everyone on our block; we've localised ourselves. I don't think there's another place on earth I'd rather be right now. We're very happy. We've just been living in Brooklyn and really committing our time to Matilda. We've just been letting it kind of consume us. We wanted to distance ourselves and we couldn't think of anything better to do than wake up to play with our child. That's the biggest gift this industry has given us, the ability to do that.'

He would have plenty of time to think about future roles during that paternity leave. Although he had passed on appearing in *Spider-Man* and also reportedly turned down the lead role in Oliver Stone's *Alexander*, Heath was poised to make appearances as two genuine iconic figures of popular culture.

One was The Joker, the crazed opponent of Batman in both the comic strip, television and the movies, where Jack Nicholson's magnificent over-the-top performance had stolen the show some years earlier. The other was a musician who had probably changed the world more than any other, folk singer Bob Dylan, whose songs had shaped the thinking of generations, from the 1960s onwards.

He would need all the rest he could get...

CHAPTER 15

MOVING OUT – AND SLEEPING PILLS

Filming of *I'm Not There* began in Montreal in the summer of 2006. Although nominally about Bob Dylan, this was far from a normal biography of the writer-singer. A number of actors played Dylan, or perhaps it would be more accurate to call them incantations of the music legend, and Heath was one of them. He didn't even get to play Dylan; he was acting out the role of an actor who was pretending to be Dylan! Among the ensemble put together by director Todd Haynes were Christian Bale and Richard Gere, with Cate Blanchett playing one of the 'Dylans'.

Heath tried to explain the somewhat extraordinary premise of the film: 'I'm one of about seven people who are kind of playing him. I'm actually playing an actor who plays in a movie as a character, and his character is a Bob Dylanesque kind of guy played by Christian Bale. So I'm

kind of playing Christian Bale, who's not playing Bob
Dylan. Michelle is actually working on it, as well. She's
shooting as we speak. And I saw Cate Blanchett the other
day on set and it's just striking. She looks like Bob Dylan,
from a distance; it's really quite remarkable. Todd is an
exciting film-maker. And everyone I've spoken with so far
has said that he's a genius and it's the most creative process
they've all been a part of. I'm really excited about it. I start
on Tuesday. I've just been rehearsing by myself in
Montreal, working on accents. I have to come up with two
accents: I have my character and his character's accent.'

He added, 'The film doesn't sum up Dylan's life or try to
explain it all. We're just representing aspects of his life
during different periods of it. I found the connection
obviously through his music. You can't help but fall in love
with his lyrics or should I say his poetry?'

In an aid to getting into character, Heath was given
photos of Dylan from the mid-1960s when the rocker spent
his time in New York City desperately trying to hide his
identity by wandering around in dark glasses. It must have
been strange for Heath to realise that four decades earlier
Dylan was experiencing the same downside of fame that
Heath was to encounter generations later.

The movie gave him an even stronger link with the music
world and shortly after filming finished he was able to
realise a dream and move into the music business when he
launched his own record label based on Los Angeles called
Masses Music Co and signed up a 17-year-old singer-
songwriter, Grace Woodroofe from Perth. Heath then

directed and shot Woodroofe's first video clip, a cover of the David Bowie song 'Quicksand'. He put his interest this way: 'I do have some wonderful distractions. I have a music label and I direct music videos and so I immerse myself in a different industry which kind of keeps acting really fresh for me. So when I do come back to acting I am excited to act again. And, like having a daughter, it is an amazingly beautiful distraction, of course.'

Very sensibly and diplomatically, he refused to 'rate' the various Dylans, but he couldn't help but rave over the performance of fellow Australian Cate Blanchett: 'Cate has given such an incredible transformation. She will really blow people away. I mean, she walks, talks, sings and smells like Bob Dylan!' He added, 'She is a brilliant actress and a wonderful person; she surprises me constantly. I saw her on her last day of shooting – we kind of high-fived each other. We were both in wigs. Her resemblance to Dylan was shocking.'

Blanchett gave her own version of the decision to cast her as one of the Dylans – it was 'bonkers', she said, adding, 'It was an incredible idea and an amazing way to conceive of telling a tale about the spirit of Bob Dylan, who was so elusive and mercurial and omnipotent to divide his persona into six different personas.'

Heath was not alone in his assessment of Cate Blanchett's performance. She gathered award after award – including an Oscar nomination for Best Supporting Actress. Indeed she won the Best Actress award at 2007's Venice Film Festival, where Heath was busy promoting the film, which was to be criticised by a few but highly praised by many more. It fell to him to accept Blanchett's award at Venice – she was unable to attend – which he did, wearing a strange outfit of grey shorts, a black waistcoat, bright yellow shirt with red-and-white striped socks and black lace-up shoes. He finished the look off with a casual backpack, dark sunglasses and a white handkerchief in the lapel of the suit jacket he wore over his waistcoat. He was smiling as he posed on the red carpet and even volunteered to take pictures of himself with the fans.

He appeared tense at the press conference for the Dylan film, however, but other interviewers found him relaxed when they were able to talk properly with him. It was all the more remarkable because there was one subject that autumn that he was not prepared to talk about – his split with Michelle Williams.

The couple had been together for three years since those first few snowy *Brokeback Mountain* scenes and the birth of Matilda seemed to cement that love. Yet it had all come to an end. Unconfirmed reports of the separation began to emerge in September 2007, although the actual break-up had occurred some time before. A few days later the confirmation came from Michelle's Australian-based father, Larry, who said: 'We have known about their troubles for a while but it's always a very difficult thing in life when these things happen. I know Heath and Michelle still care about each other deeply and are very committed to being great parents to their daughter.' He blamed pressures of work for their break-up, saying: 'You can never be stunned by what happens in Hollywood – I learned that when we were dealing with Michelle's career when she was younger. Michelle was grown up at 16 and, just like Heath, her life has had an extremely fast pace to it. I feel tremendously for her and for him, and hope they will find what they want in life.'

It was sensational news.

Heath had always been protective of his privacy and many of his confrontations with the media were based on his justifiable feeling that he did not have to have every moment of his private life acted out in the public arena. But after meeting and falling in love with Michelle he had been only too pleased to talk about her and the effect the young actress and their baby had on his life. It seemed a classic case of young love. The pair even had a mainly female audience at a recording of the *Oprah Winfrey Show* practically swooning over their affection for each other.

Neither side was prepared to go public with the exact reasons for the ending of the romance although reports at the time suggested the discord had been there for longer than many people realised. It was only later that details, many of them unsubstantiated rumours linked to Heath's alleged behaviour, began to emerge. As traumatic as the ending of the relationship undoubtedly was, neither of them was prepared to run and hide. Michelle was spotted out with some girlfriends in New York while Heath was in Venice, and on his return to the Big Apple he was immediately linked with Danish supermodel Helena Christensen, 10 years his senior.

The *New York Post* said, 'they couldn't keep their hands off each other' while dining at Manhattan eatery Wakiya. 'They were making out throughout the dinner and later, he even held her bag for her as she did interviews,' one source told the paper. Afterwards the couple headed to the Soho Grand hotel and then on to an after-party for Heath's ex-girlfriend Naomi Watts' new film *Eastern Promises*.

Heath wasn't the first Australian to make a mark with the 38-year-old former model, who used to date the late INXS rocker Michael Hutchence. The same newspaper, who by now was monitoring his movements closely, also linked him with his *Four Feathers* co-star Kate Hudson and said that he had exchanged phone numbers with old flame Heather Graham after meeting her at a party. Heath, who had moved out of the home he shared with Michelle into an apartment in Manhattan's SoHo, was also said to be keen on model-turned-actress Gemma Ward – like Heath a native of Perth, who was now living in New York, the paper claimed. It went so far as to say that he was 'following Gemma around everywhere.'

Australian newspapers were to take up the theme and when the couple were back home in Australia for Christmas with their families they were spotted together going to the movies and on Boxing Day they were alongside each other at Creatures Loft restaurant in Fremantle, near their home city. 'They weren't all over each other but they were sitting together and looked like they were together,' a source told Australian journalists. Restaurant manager William Wood was quoted as saying, 'They had a very good time. It's pretty obvious they're an item.'

Heath and Ward, 20, had spent one evening in the reclining deckchairs in the front row of Perth's picturesque Camelot Outdoor Cinema watching the movie *Two Days in Paris* and Sophie Ward, Gemma's sister and a fellow model, noticed that Heath, despite being back home, could not relax. Sophie said he was distressed about his split with Michelle and also being away from his daughter, who had accompanied her mother on a filming trip to Sweden.

'We went to the movies and just did normal stuff… but he was a bit edgy. He couldn't really relax,' said Sophie. Heath drank only Diet Coke. 'He smoked cigarettes but that's about it. He said he was very committed to not drinking alcohol. He was travelling so much and I think he was just frustrated with it all.'

The 'sightings' of Heath and Gemma only emerged some time after Christmas. That holiday period was to be the last in his beloved Perth. Compared with some of his visits to Australia since becoming famous it was remarkably low-key – something he appreciated in that it gave him time to relax with his family during a break in his hectic schedule. He escaped media harassment and took the highly unusual step of ringing the film editor of the local newspaper in Perth, Mark Naglazas. The phone was switched off, but when he turned it on, Naglazas heard the following message: 'It's Heath again, Katie's brother. Listen, if I don't catch you 'cause I leave soon, basically I don't have anyone else to call and I thought as I've spoken to you before, I thought I'd ring up and just send some thanks out there to the peeps at the *West Australian* and the *Sunday Times* and everyone in Perth in general.

'I don't know whether it's a conscious thing or an unconscious thing, giving me space and respecting my privacy. It's just been awesome and I've had the most beautiful time back here and being able to see all my friends and family, let alone the press and the people within the community of Perth, it's been so lovely. It's really enabled me to be a boy again from home and feel like I'd never left. Like I said, I'm not sure whether it's a conscious decision on the paper's part or not to kind of give me this space, but they have and I truly, truly thank them for it and it makes my life a life when I come back here. I know you're probably not the man to print this but you can certainly pass this on to your compatriots and that's really it, just sending my love and thanks to the city of Perth because it's truly been an incredibly therapeutic and a much-needed trip home and just that little touch has made it all that more special to me. I hope you had a wonderful Christmas and certainly a Happy New Year, if I don't speak to you before I leave. I will no doubt be talking to you probably next year when *Batman* comes out – and *Batman* goes down! In fact, thanks for listening to my long-winded message. Like I said, feel free to use it and pass it on to someone who can type it out and thanks again, OK, bye bye!'

That reference to the Joker role was a poignant one. The Batman film, *The Dark Knight*, directed by

Christopher Nolan was to be the last he completed and the strain of perfecting his role played a vital role in the events that lay ahead. Not too long before that happy trip to Perth he was giving interviews to promote the Dylan film, but the conversation invariably got round to his role as The Joker, due for release in the summer of 2008.

Heath had added some more tattoos to his collection by the time he gave the interviews: a dragonfly had gone onto his upper right arm just below a planets tattoo (the sun, moon and earth). Even Heath was forced to admit, 'They all have meanings but f**k, I don't know why I keep covering myself with these things.'

Jack Nicholson made The Joker role famous in Tim Burton's 1989 film – Heath 'loved, loved' his performance – but even Michael Caine, who was in the new movie, was moved to comment, 'Jack was like a really scary, nasty old uncle with a funny face. Heath is like the most murderous psychopath you've ever seen on the screen, he's fantastic.'

Heath put it slightly differently: 'I wouldn't have thought of me [as The Joker], either. But it's obviously not going to be what Jack Nicholson did. It's going to be more nuanced and dark and more along the lines of *A Clockwork Orange* kind of feel. Which is, I think, what the comic book was after: less about his laugh and more about his eyes.' He was happy to say, though, 'It is actually the most fun I have had with any character. It just clicked. It was easy and nasty, bloody and vicious.' He added, 'I was a fan of the comic book character. Somewhere inside of me, I kind of knew instantly that I wanted to do it. I didn't feel like I had to search for it. I felt like I had a plan of attack with it. That usually dictates whether I want to do something or not – if I have an understanding of it straightaway.'

Although the film was 'the most fun I've ever had with a character and the most fun I probably ever will have,' he tellingly added, 'even though at the end of the day I was absolutely wrecked.' His Joker 'has zero empathy' for Batman or anyone else in Gotham City, he said, and Heath's intention from the start was to be a fierce, scary Joker: 'He's really full of surprises but I can say that I wanted him to be very sinister. I actually hate comic-book movies. But I thought what Nolan did with *Batman Begins* was actually really good – really well directed – and Christian Bale was really great in it. The Joker is a pure anarchist. I definitely have a different take on him. He's going to be really sinister and it's going to be less about his laugh and his pranks. I'm not really thinking about the commercial consequences – maybe I should be. I can just tell you I love to dress up and to wear a mask.

'At this point, it's just an exciting next step. Before I got into the industry, I never imagined I'd have anywhere near the money I have now. I don't need any more. It's not that I don't want the money, it's just that I would have been really happy sitting on a beach or surfing every morning. I never had money, and I was very happy without it. When I die, my money's not gonna come with me. My movies will live on – for people to judge what I was as a person. I just want to stay curious.'

He may not have been keen to talk about his separation

from Michelle, but he was more than happy to relate the impact little Matilda had on his life: 'Having a child changes every aspect of your life – for the better, of course. The sacrifices are large but what you get in return is even bigger than the sacrifices you make. I feel in a sense ready to die because you are living on in your child. Not literally, not ready to die – but you know, that sort of feeling in a profound way. So fatherhood has changed me as an artist because I feel things on a deeper level. I think my performances will grow simultaneously.'

The Joker role would obviously be a lucrative one so it was remarkable for Heath to say, 'I'm not good at future planning – I don't plan at all. I don't know what I'm doing tomorrow. I don't have a day planner and I don't have a diary. I completely live in the now – not in the past, not in the future.'

As an actor he was always enthusiastic about working with good directors and he lamented that many of those he admired and wanted to work with were no longer around: 'Look, most of them are dead: Fellini, Cassavettes, Bob Fosse, Stanley Kubrick... I would have loved to work with them. I would love to work with many people who are around, but they're not lining up just yet. Terrence Malick is one person who comes to mind. I would love to be in one of his visual poems.'

One of the last interviews he gave was to the *New York Times*, in which he said of the Dylan role: 'I stressed out a little too much.' Even more revealing were the comments he made about his work and the strain it was putting on him, his Joker being, 'a psychopathic, mass-murdering, schizophrenic clown with zero empathy.' Then he added, in a remark that was to appear countless times around the world just a few weeks later: 'Last week I probably slept an average of two hours a night. I couldn't stop thinking. My body was exhausted, and my mind was still going.'

The paper reported: 'One night he took an Ambien [a sedative used to combat insomnia] which failed to work so he took a second one and fell into a stupor, only to wake up an hour later, his mind still racing.' It added later, 'Even as he spoke, Mr. Ledger was hard-pressed to keep still. He got up and poured more coffee. He stepped outside into the courtyard and smoked a cigarette. He shook his hair out from under its hood, put a rubber band around it, took out the rubber band, put on a hat, took off the hat, put the hood back up. He went outside and had another cigarette.'

The lengthy article concluded by quoting Heath as saying: 'People always feel compelled to sum you up, to presume that they have you and can describe you. That's fine. But there are many stories inside of me and a lot I want to achieve outside of one flat note.'

The thoughts he expressed during that interview in London, in the winter of 2007, and the physical state he described were to be an indication of the terrible events in store, a chilling foretaste of what lay ahead...

CHAPTER 16

DEATH IN SOHO

After his split with Michelle Williams, Heath was frequently seen out and about in New York's trendiest bars and clubs and his name was linked with a string of beautiful young women. Newspapers and magazines in America, Australia and the UK all said that he was seeing troubled *Freaky Friday* actress Lindsay Lohan. Frequently in and out of rehab, Lohan had also been in trouble with the police for various driving offences and being in possession of cocaine when they questioned her; she wasn't alone in having her name alongside Heath's, though.

The following story appeared in the *New York Post* on 12 November 2007 and this time the woman headlined with Heath was his co-star from *The Four Feathers*, Kate Hudson, who like him was 'free' of a romantic partner at the time: 'Kate Hudson has moved on to an actual movie star. Hudson, having dumped funny man (Dax) Shepard, was linked to Dane Cook, but Thursday night she only had eyes for Heath Ledger. Spies at Beatrice Inn said they spent their evening at the trendy watering hole "kissing and making out." A rep for Hudson said, "This is absolutely untrue. They ran into each other and chatted briefly, but that was the extent of it." But our spy insists on the liplock.'

Given the state of his relationship with Michelle it probably wasn't too surprising that Heath, a handsome, rich young film star, should have attractive female companions. He knew that relationships change and perhaps his parents' divorce all those years before had impacted on him and his commitment to long-term partnerships in a way that even he was not able to properly assess.

Whether or not it was true that he had bonded closely with Hudson, what was indisputable was that he was certainly a regular at the exclusive Beatrice Inn, a former speakeasy complete with doorman to keep out the not-so stylish near the vast apartment at 421 Broome Street in SoHo, Manhattan that he had moved into in the September. With three bedrooms, an office, two and half bathrooms, a laundry room and balcony, it occupied the entire fourth floor: 4,400 square feet – ten times the size of some Manhattan homes. Heath was paying $24.000 (£12,000) a month to live in one of the Big Apple's coolest neighbourhoods. When he moved in, it was unfurnished – and virtually to stay that way, apart from skateboards dotted around. One visitor described it as being more like a 'crash pad' than a wealthy film star's home.

He did equip one room in the loft for when Matilda stayed, however. It resembled her room in the Brooklyn home he had recently vacated and he bought her a large stuffed sheep so that she could lie on it while watching television. No doubt he missed his child because in one of the last interviews he was to give he summed up his feelings about being a father when he said, 'I think you also look at death differently. It's like a Catch-22. Like, I feel good about dying now because I feel like I'm alive in her, you know? But at the same hand, you don't want to die because you want to be around for the rest of her life. That's kind of, like, an interesting kind of little set-up.'

Michelle also gave an interview in which she summarised her feelings about the split: 'Obviously so much has changed for me in the last few months that I don't really have an idea of what my life is going to be. I thought I knew certain things and it turned out I didn't, so I don't really try and anticipate so much any more. I'm not making any bets on the future. I love domestic life,' she said, adding, 'There's been a lot going on in my personal life and… it's like I'm re-emerging back into the world or something.'

And in a statement that echoed Naomi Watts' feelings of some years earlier, she welcomed the reduction in the attention of paparazzi now that Heath was no longer by her side: 'When you're in a relationship with somebody who is also a public personality, it doubles the attention from the media. When you minus that equation, it's just less enticing. That's been a real bonus, the plus side of the break-up.'

Meanwhile, Heath's schedule was as busy as ever and by his own admission the Joker role had been, 'hard stamina-wise, a high level of energy was needed every day.' Nevertheless, after his Christmas break in Perth he soon had to return to London to continue work on what proved to be his last film, *The Imaginarium of Doctor Parnassus*, directed by Terry Gilliam – with whom he had hit it off with so well during *The Brothers Grimm*. Of course the trip to Australia and the work in London meant that he was away from Matilda for long periods.

This time his co-stars were veteran Christopher Plummer, a living part of film legend through his role as Captain von Trapp in *The Sound of Music*, and the gravel-voiced singer-actor Tom Watts. The script by Gilliam, co-written with his long-time collaborator Charles McKeown, was typical of the one-time Python's work. Set in the present day, Doctor Parnassus (Plummer) has made a deal with the Devil (Watts) and because of this the audience at his travelling show can go through his magical mirror into an imaginary world. As part of the deal, the Devil eventually targets Plummer's daughter, played by supermodel model Lily Cole, and the troupe are joined by an outsider, Tony (Heath) to rescue her.

During filming, Heath stayed in a house in Islington, north London, which often meant working up to 15 hours on some days. Co-star Plummer said, 'We all caught colds because we were shooting outside on horrible, damp nights; what's more, he [Heath] was saying all the time, "Dammit, I can't sleep!" and he was taking all these pills.'

On Saturday, 19 January 2008, his London filming was over and Heath jetted back to New York to spend some time there before filming moved on to Canada. He was tired from the journey and still feeling under the weather; in addition he could not see his beloved Matilda as she was out of the country with her mother, who was also filming. He was spotted buying coffees at two of his regular haunts near his new home, his iPod on all the time. On the Sunday night he again went to The Beatrice Inn and drank late into the night. He wore a ski mask and a hood for his evening out, perhaps to keep out the chill – he was still suffering from a cold – or maybe this was to preserve his anonymity.

On the Monday he stopped for a meal with two women companions at Angelica Kitchen, a vegetarian restaurant in the East Village, and he also made plans to go out on the Tuesday evening with his tattoo artist pal Scott Campbell. Campbell had a parlour in Brooklyn and had done several of Heath's tattoos, including a recent 'M' for Matilda. One of the people who kept in constant touch with Heath was his friend and director of *The Four Feathers*, Shekhar Kapur. The two often discussed further projects, including one in which a television reporter (to be played by Heath) turned a war in a third-world country into a kind of 'reality TV show' for the benefit of his Western audiences.

On the Monday night the director telephoned Heath and had what was probably the young Australian's last conversation. 'He said he could not see me that night but wanted to meet the next day. He made me promise I would call him in the morning and wake him up,' Kapur recalled. 'He was completely jet-lagged, but he was looking forward to the next day. We were talking about meeting up and laughing about synchronicity because I had booked a massage for him at three o'clock, and he'd booked one for himself at the same time. He told me to call him in the morning. I said, "I won't disturb you if you're tired." But he said, "No, call me. Wake me up, and we'll meet." There was nothing he said that gave me the impression he was depressed.'

The director phoned the next morning, but got no reply. The final chapter of Heath's life was beginning...

At 12.30p.m. on Tuesday, 22 January, housekeeper Teresa Solomon, 56, arrived for her once-a-week visit to Heath's apartment. She let herself in with a key. There was a note on the refrigerator door saying that masseuse Diane Lee Wolozin would be arriving later to massage Heath. The door to his bedroom was closed and at 1p.m. Solomon entered to change a light bulb in the adjacent bathroom and she heard him snoring. 'The last time I saw him he was lying down on his face. I didn't think anything was wrong; I thought he was sleeping,' she said. A further 1 hour 45 minutes passed before the 40-year-old masseuse arrived at 2.45 p.m., 15 minutes early for her 3p.m. appointment, and the two women chatted briefly, filling in the time.

At 3.10p.m. Wolozin called Heath on his mobile phone but there was no answer. She then decided to knock on the door; still no response. The masseuse went into the bedroom and began setting up her massage table. Heath was lying naked, face down, at the foot of the bed, with a sheet up to his shoulders. He was unconscious and she could not wake him; he was also cold to the touch. Pills were strewn about the linen and there was a pill bottle next to his body.

Then came one of the most mysterious parts in the chain of events that was quickly unfolding. Instead of telephoning the 911 emergency services, she obtained the phone number of a friend of Heath's – actress Mary-Kate Olsen – from his mobile phone and decided to call her instead. She was later quoted in one New York newspaper as doing this because she 'did not want a media circus.' Wolozin knew both Heath and Olsen and was aware they were friends.

Mary-Kate Olsen, 21, one half of the Olsen twins, a pair of actresses well known from television work in America since their childhood days, was in California when she received the call. An un-named police source was later to tell the New York media that the couple had been dating and, irrespective of the exact nature of their relationship, the actress was to figure prominently in the bizarre sequence that followed. This is the dramatic timetable – pieced together by police from Heath's telephone records and from interviews with the parties involved – as the nightmare events began to unfold:

3.17 p.m.: At last the alarm was raised by Wolozin; not to the 911 operator, only to Olsen. 'Heath is unconscious, I don't know what to do!' the frightened

Wolozin screamed in her first call to the actress. 'I'm sending my private security there,' Olsen replied. The call lasted 49 seconds.

3.20 p.m.: After again trying again to wake Heath, Wolozin made another panicked call. 'I think he may be dead, I'm calling 911!' she said. 'I already have people coming over,' Olsen replied. That call lasted 1 minute and 39 seconds.

3.24 p.m.: The masseuse makes a third phone call to Olsen. The call lasted 21 seconds and then finally at 3.26 p.m. she eventually called 911. The emergency operator gave her advice on how to perform CPR (cardiopulmonary resuscitation), a combination of mouth-to-mouth resuscitation and chest compressions that can restore circulation of oxygen-rich blood to the brain.

3.33 p.m.: Paramedics arrived and went up to the apartment in an elevator with Olsen's security guards, who were also now on the scene. They did not let the security guards into the bedroom where Heath lay. His bed was surrounded by an assortment of bottles and pills.

3.34 p.m.: Wolozin made a final call to Olsen. The duration is not known.

3.36 p.m.: Heath Ledger was pronounced dead by the medical team.

Minutes later, police arrived and they found bottles of 6 different pills – 2 for anxiety, 2 for insomnia and 2 for pain

– in his bedroom and bathroom. Heath had prescriptions for them all, some issued in Europe. The 6 prescription drugs included an antihistamine, anti-anxiety drugs Xanax and Valium, as well as the sleep aid Ambien, which a few months earlier, he had admitted taking when talking to a journalist.

A rolled-up $20 bill was also on the floor near the bed. Rolled-up bills are often used to snort coke or other drugs, but a toxicology test found no drugs on the bill. There was no evidence of alcohol use and no illegal drugs were found. Nor was there any suicide note.

NYPD Sgt Carlos Nieves said, 'He looked like a hundred corpses I've seen before; he looked pale. You see the body and you try to imagine what he looked like in pictures and movies.'

Within a short time the following news story was flashing around the world. The message, from an international news agency, gave out the few brief facts they had:

Actor Heath Ledger was found dead in his Manhattan apartment on Tuesday, possibly of a drug overdose, New York City police said. The Australian-born Ledger, 28, who starred in *Brokeback Mountain*, was found dead by a housekeeper at his apartment in the trendy SoHo neighbourhood, police spokesman (Deputy Police Commissioner) Paul Browne said. 'We are investigating the possibility of an overdose,' Browne said.

It was the briefest of stories but soon an avalanche of copy reached newspapers around the world, with radio and television giving live reports of the discovery of Heath's body. The area around his new home – and his old one in Brooklyn too – was besieged by press, cameramen and TV crews.

At 6.28 p.m. his body was brought downstairs and out into the cold New York air. Immediately the dark night was lit by the flashes of cameras and mobile phone cameras and the crowd of journalists and back-up crews swelled to 800 with members of the public. Some of them were fans moved to tears by the news; others just attracted by all the commotion. Australian tourist Jenelle Cleary, 29, from the Melbourne suburb of Reservoir, was there and the tragedy reminded her of the early passing of INXS frontman Michael Hutchence, a decade ago: 'I'm a fan, that's why I had to come down. I can't believe it. He's just so young – it's like Michael Hutchence, same feeling and just so tragic.'

Another Australian, Catherine Counihan, a production manager working in SoHo, said: 'He's the same age as me as well, and I'm just trying to make it out here in the same way in America and it's so disappointing that a life could be lost so young. He was a good Aussie actor who was doing well out here and it's a shame.' New York drama student Jessica Faar, 19, was one of many who took flowers to the scene of the tragedy: 'It's very reminiscent of James Dean. It's just sad; it just seems like people are dying younger and younger – they do not get to flourish before they become superstars.'

Others with flowers were Harlem flatmates Lesleigh Valette, 18, and Ileana Diaz, 16, who got on the subway and came to SoHo to see for themselves if the story was true. 'I'm a huge Heath Ledger fan. I wouldn't be here otherwise, it's cold,' drama student Ms Valette said. 'I didn't believe it – I still can't, to be honest.'

Two paramedics pushed the trolley with Heath strapped to it inside a black plastic body bag across the sidewalk and loaded it into the waiting white Medical Examiner's office van. Meanwhile, cameras flashed at demonic speed.

Tragically Heath's family in Australia knew nothing of the incident until it was broken to them by the media, a heartbreaking way to learn of the death of a loved one. His father, Kim, issued a short statement: 'Heath's family confirm the very tragic, untimely and accidental passing of our dearly loved son, brother and doting father of Matilda. He was found peacefully asleep in his New York apartment by his housekeeper at 3.30 p.m. US time.

'We would like to thank our friends and everyone around the world for their well wishes and kind thoughts at this time. Heath has touched so many people on so many different levels during his short life but few had the pleasure of truly knowing him. He was a down-to-earth, generous, kind-hearted, life-loving, unselfish individual who was extremely inspirational to many. Please now respect our family's need to grieve and come to terms with our loss privately, thank you.'

In another statement, Mara Buxbaum, Heath's publicist, said: 'We are all deeply saddened and shocked by this accident. This is an extremely difficult time for his loved ones and we are asking the media to please respect the family's privacy and avoid speculation until the facts are known.'

When he heard the news, Shekhar Kapur said that he had tried, as promised, to contact his friend that day but 'Little did I know that his soul had already left his body.' He was not the only one to call on that terrible day. Helena Christensen, 39, who had been romantically linked with Heath but insisted they were just 'friends' revealed she was on her way to visit him when she learned of his death: 'I am beyond sad at this point. I had just left him a message and heard his voice on the machine. He was such a special and genuine person, so extraordinarily talented.' It was to be one of the first of many tributes.

An initial 90-minute autopsy to discover exactly how Heath died was carried out, but New York City Medical Examiner's office spokeswoman Ellen Borakove revealed, 'The autopsy is inconclusive. We have to do additional testing which will include toxicology and tissue testing. It will take about 10 days.' His body was transferred to the Frank E. Campbell funeral chapel on Manhattan's Upper East Side.

But alongside the praise and the heartfelt messages of condolence from those who knew him and those who did not, were words of not so kind a nature. There was speculation that Heath's depression at not being with Matilda as much as he wanted, allied to his workload, had been too much for him. Perhaps his death was not an accident? Such gossip was fed by stories pointing out a strange video of him 'drowning' himself, set to a song from late singer-songwriter Nick Drake, who committed suicide in 1974. The black-and-white clip, which Heath shot and edited, was included in a multi-media installation, 'A Place To Be,' devoted to Drake the previous summer at Seattle's Bumbershoot festival. It was also on display during a celebration of the same name in Los Angeles in October 2007.

In the film, Heath turns the camera on himself while Drake's 'Black Eyed Dog' plays. At its conclusion, he drowns himself in a bathtub. 'Black Eyed Dog' was allegedly the last song Drake, whose music Heath had admired, wrote before overdosing on the antidepressant amitriptyline. Indeed, the *Sunday Times* wrote, 'Like Drake he was found in his bed at home after taking prescription antidepressants, which has given rise to suicide rumours' – these suggestions were immediately rebutted by his family, still stunned at their loss.

His uncle Neil Bell insisted the actor would not kill himself: 'Someone doesn't take their life when they make an appointment for a massage. Ever since he was a boy, his dream was to be an actor. The last thing he'd do is throw his dream away.'

No sooner had Heath's death reached the shocked world than numerous 'friends' and 'sources' began to be quoted in newspapers and magazines, giving what they saw as a different picture of the last few months of his life. The *Daily Mirror* in London reported one such source as saying: 'He frequently seemed out of it. Heath had serious problems with drugs, including cocaine and heroin.' The newspaper added, 'But friends said he was trying to clean up his act: "At a party in December, he was doing his best to avoid people doing drugs. But that didn't seem to work, as he was spotted partaking later."'

The *New York Daily News* said: 'Friends told investigators that Williams booted Ledger from the Brooklyn home they shared with their 2-year-old daughter, Matilda, because of a drug problem that only got worse after he left, a police source said.'

There was a story in America's *US* magazine that in 2006 Michelle had tried to persuade Heath to enter rehab and actually drove him to Promises Treatment Center in Malibu. According to the report, he refused to check in; instead he changed her mind by pledging to become clean. Mara Buxbaum, who also represented Michelle, immediately denied the story, saying, 'Much of the tabloid reporting is inaccurate. This fabricated story of Michelle Williams attempting to bring Heath Ledger to rehab is just one lie among many. The speculation is heinous. Let this family grieve privately.'

Back in Perth, the Ledger family, still horrified by the news, was forced to begin making arrangements for the 11,000 mile trip to New York. Michelle, too, was grief-stricken when the news was broken to her in Trollhattan in Sweden, where she was shooting scenes for the film *Mammoth*, accompanied by the couple's daughter, Matilda. She made immediate plans to return to New York and her mother Carla and best friend actress Busy Philipps, godmother to the little girl, were to meet her at her Brooklyn home.

Flowers, bouquets and tributes were already being left near the family home in Brooklyn, near where Heath had helped write 'Matilda' in wet cement in happier times and the apartment where he was found dead. They were even laid on the other side of the country at his 'Treehouse' home in Los Angeles.

Even as plans were being made for the funeral and genuinely grieving family and friends were trying to cope with such an unexpected loss, the stories of Heath's behaviour, allegedly fuelled by drugs, were growing. One of the most distressing took several days to surface. It was based on a video filmed at one of Heath's favourite hotels, the Château Marmont in Los Angeles, where comedian John Belushi had died years before, and it showed Heath partying with a group of 'friends'. Several television programmes declined to broadcast the film out of respect for the Ledger family, but its details soon surfaced in newspapers and on websites around the globe.

An example of the coverage it received was in England's mass-selling *News of the World*, who also posted the party footage images on their website. The newspaper stated: 'These pictures show tragic movie star Heath Ledger revelling in a debauched drugs party where he snorted lines of cocaine.' The story added that Michelle and Matilda were asleep elsewhere in the hotel and quoted an anonymous fellow party-goer as saying,

'So instead of enjoying his newfound role as a dad he spends hours with a bunch of cokehead nobodies, getting off his head on drugs.'

The footage was said to have been taken two years earlier, when Matilda was just a few months old, after the Screen Actors Guild Awards. After meeting up with a group of people in the hotel bar Heath was said to have gone back to one of the £1,500-a-night bungalows at the hotel, where he allegedly partied for three hours. At one stage he can be heard on the soundtrack saying, 'I'm going to be in serious s**t with my girlfriend... we had our baby three months ago and I'm not supposed to be here.'

Drinking beer from a bottle he added: 'I used to smoke five joints a day,' bizarrely adding that the habit went back 20 years. Then he referred to his daughter and said, 'She's amazing: we called her Matilda Rose, it's an old-school name.' He went on, 'I started a record company with Ben Harper [his singing friend] and when she was born he wrote a lullaby for her. It was pretty cool.'

A witness to the party was quoted as saying: 'When the coke eventually dried up Heath stumbled back to his own room. He was in a complete state and totally high on drugs.'

Around the time details of the hotel video were surfacing, the *New York Post* reported: 'Michelle Williams was forced to boot him out of their Brooklyn home, The Post has learned.' Quoting an unnamed member of Heath's circle, the 'friend' said: 'She couldn't take it any more. Heath wouldn't show up for two to three days, and all of a sudden he would show up on her doorstep, an absolute wreck... He was partying, doing drugs. She didn't like the company he was keeping. She gave him an ultimatum... and threatened to get custody of the girl. He wanted to make it work, but it was this scene he was wrapped up in. Was he an addict? Yeah.'

In the midst of such allegations, Michelle Williams broke her silence and issued a statement that was agonisingly simple, yet with great depth of feeling: 'Please respect our need to grieve privately. I am heartbroken. I am the mother of the most tender-hearted, high-spirited, beautiful little girl who is the spitting image of her father,' she said. 'All that I can cling to is his presence inside her that reveals itself every day. His family and I watch Matilda as she whispers to trees, hugs animals, and takes steps two at a time, and we know that he is with us still. She will be brought up with the best memories of him.'

Mary-Kate Olsen had also spoken, albeit very briefly, about her feelings for Heath. She had met him some two years earlier but they had become closer after his split with Michelle. *People* magazine described their relationship in the following words: 'They had a bond that was based on partying. They just had the same sensibility.' Her short statement said, 'Heath was a friend. His death is a tragic loss. My thoughts are with his family during this very difficult time.'

Police said they had no plans to interview the one-time child star. They had spoken to the housekeeper and the masseuse, as well as paramedics and Olsen's security guards, and considered there was no need to talk to Olsen herself. Deputy Commissioner Paul Browne dismissed any controversy: 'The detectives felt they had enough from the witnesses at the scene,' he stated. 'The detectives made a determination that they had enough information.'

Police thought that death had occurred between approximately 1 p.m. and 2.45 p.m., which meant Heath would have been dead before the first call to Olsen. Also, there was no sign of any foul play – to all intents and purposes it seemed as though a terrible accident had taken place. That verdict was confirmed a few days later when the full autopsy report was released, revealing the fatal cocktail of prescription drugs – so-called 'polypharmacy' – that led to his death. Taken in small doses and in isolation they would not have harmed him, but together they had the capability to be fatal.

The full details emerged on Wednesday, 6 February 2008 when it was officially revealed that Heath Ledger had died accidentally 'from the abuse of prescription medications' – specifically, 6 kinds of painkillers, sleeping pills and anti-anxiety drugs. Spokeswoman Ellen Borakove said death occurred from 'acute intoxication' caused by the combined effects of the six drugs.

Among the drugs found in Heath's system were two widely prescribed narcotics: oxycodone, the main ingredient in the prescription drug OxyContin, and hydrocodone, the principal pain reliever in the prescription drug Vicodin. In addition there were three anti-anxiety medications: diazepam (the generic name for Valium) alprazolam (commonly known as Xanax) and temazepam, sold under the brand name Restoril and often prescribed as a sleep medication. The drug doxylamine was also found in his system. It is an ingredient in some over-the-counter sleeping pills and is also marketed in some non-prescription cold medicines that contain decongestants. The Medical Examiner's office provided only the generic names of the drugs found in his bloodstream, so it was not known exactly what forms of the drugs (brand names) he took before he died.

The statement read:

> Mr. Heath Ledger died as the result of acute intoxication by the combined effects of oxycodone, hydrocodone, diazepam, temazepam, alprazolam, and doxylamine. We have concluded that the manner of death is accident, resulting from the abuse of prescription medications.

Ms Borakove would not say how much of each drug had turned up in Heath's bloodstream. She said such concentrations were not normally made public, although the amounts were included in the information given to a person's family after an autopsy. Nor would she say if any one drug contributed more than another to his death: 'It's the combination of the drugs that caused the problem, not necessarily too much of any particular drug. All these drugs have a cumulative effect on the body.'

After the release of the medical findings, Kim Ledger issued a statement on behalf of his family:

We remain humble as parents and a family, among millions of people worldwide who may have suffered the tragic loss of a child. Few can understand the hollow, wrenching, and enduring agony parents silently suffer when a child predeceases them. Today's results put an end to speculation, but our son's beautiful spirit and enduring memory will forever remain in our hearts. While no medications were taken in excess, we learned today the combination of doctor-prescribed drugs proved lethal for our boy. Heath's accidental death serves as a caution to the hidden dangers of combining prescription medication, even at low dosage. Our family enjoyed an extremely happy, two-week visit with Heath just prior to the New Year. Those recent precious days will stay with us forever. We as a family feel privileged to have some of his amazing magic moments captured in film. To most of the world Heath was an actor of immeasurable talent and promise. To those who knew him personally, Heath was a consummate artist whose passions also included photography, music, chess and directing. We knew Heath as a loving father, as our devoted son, and as a loyal and generous brother and friend. We treasure our beautiful granddaughter Matilda (to our dear Michelle) as well as an unbelievably wonderful network of close friends, forever, around the world. Families rarely experience the uplifting, warm and massive outpouring of grief and support as have we, from every corner of the planet. This has deeply and profoundly touched our hearts and lives. We are eternally grateful. At this moment we respectfully request the worldwide media allow us time to grieve privately, without the intrusions associated with press and photography.

Meanwhile, the federal Drug Enforcement Administration (DEA) was investigating where the drugs came from and issued subpoenas to the Medical Examiner's office for information about Heath's case. As is customary whenever death by drug overdose occurs, the Federal Agency was seeking to determine whether the drugs had been legally prescribed by a doctor for a medical condition – or if any were illegally dispensed. The Agency was also working with police to obtain the original police reports about the death.

Drug Enforcement Administration spokeswoman Rogene Waite said the DEA was looking at 'all kinds of issues related to the drugs themselves and whether there were any violations of the Controlled Substances Act. We know it's extraordinarily dangerous for people to try to self-medicate and to mix drugs that they may have in their medicine chest. It's like having a loaded gun.'

One of the factors which most concerned the DEA was the use of the oxycodone, an opium derivative known as 'Hillbilly Heroin', responsible for many deaths in the US. In excess it provides a sensation not unlike heroin and its use and abuse by poor people in the Appalachian Mountain range has resulted in its grim nickname. It could be deadly – and often was. And now it seemed that it had played a part, although no one could say exactly how great, in the death of one of the most glamorous figures of the film world – no longer did it just belong to Hillbillies.

CHAPTER 17

TEARS, TRIBUTES – AND SMILES AT SUNSET

That terrible Tuesday of 22 January 2008 hadn't even drawn to a close before the tributes to Heath Ledger began. They came from the famous and the fans, those who knew him and those who simply wished they did – but now knew they never would.

One of the first to praise him was Mel Gibson, the star Heath had often been tipped to emulate and perhaps even surpass, a compliment and prediction he always took with a large pinch of salt and a small dose of good-humoured scepticism. 'I had such great hope for him... to lose his life at such a young age is a tragic loss. My thoughts and prayers are with him and his family,' Gibson said.

The undisputed 'Queen' of the Australian acting world, Nicole Kidman, Heath's old flame Naomi Watts' lifelong friend, echoed that mood when she said his death was 'a tragedy. My heart goes out to his family.' Another major actress from Australia, his much admired co-star in the *Dylan* film, Cate Blanchett, commented: 'This is such a sad event. I admired Heath enormously. He was such a sensitive and committed and daring actor. This is truly a tragedy. I send my condolences to his family and friends and colleagues.' Blanchett, who was nominated for an Oscar for her role in the film, was to add later, when she collected an Independent Spirit Award for independent film-makers: 'To probably one of the most beautiful independent spirits of all, this is for him.'

At the same ceremony the film's director Todd Haynes admitted he was 'shattered' by Ledger's 'inconceivable absence.' He said, 'We all loved him so dearly. He really was unlike anybody I've ever known, giving up of himself less like an actor than a creative partner.' In addition, he paid tribute to his hidden talents as a director of 'diverse music videos,' and revealed Heath was in the process of making his directorial debut on a feature film just before he died: 'He had just started circulating a feature script that he was planning to direct – an adaptation of *The Queen's Gambit* by Walter Tevis. I have no doubt he would have made an astounding director... I treasure the time we shared on this film and the love and talent that he gave so freely.'

At the same ceremony actress Patricia Clarkson said: 'Anyone who has seen the film *I'm Not There* will remember the line, "Live in your own times, child." As actors, we were lucky to live in Heath's times. We only wish they could have been longer.'

The man who, as much as anyone, could claim to have elevated Ledger to the status of a true star, *Brokeback Mountain* director Ang Lee, said, 'Working with Heath was one of the purest joys of my life. He brought to the role of Ennis more than any of us could have imagined – a thirst for life, for love, and for truth, and a vulnerability that made everyone who knew him love him. His death is heartbreaking.'

One of his co-stars in *Candy*, actor Geoffrey Rush, stated, 'This is such a sad event. I admired Heath enormously; he was such a sensitive and committed and daring actor. This truly is a tragedy.'

Larry Williams, Michelle Williams' father, spoke from the heart when he said: 'Tennyson got it right in the poem when he described someone as having died at a young age but burning the candles at both ends, and oh what a beautiful flame he made.'

Robert Zordan, headmaster of Heath's old school, Guildford Grammar School, said the actor had never forgotten his schooldays or the friends he had made in Perth: 'One of the great things about him as a person was that with all the stardom and with all the lights that were focused on him, it was with a degree of humility and loyalty that he remained very, very closely in touch with many of his peers from his particular year group. I know for example that when his friends from schooldays were in New York he would be a very, very generous and loyal host, often putting them up in his own home. He was a very skilled hockey player and ultimately was selected to represent the state in the under-17 hockey squad. In the latter part of his secondary schooling years he discovered, with a tremendous passion, a love of the creative and performing arts and specifically drama. It was there really that he left his mark in the school. He wasn't a tearaway in any shape or form, he was one of those people that when sport was important to him sometimes the academics faded into the background. When he got locked and loaded into something, like drama, it was drama 100 per cent.' Zordan said that naturally the school's students would be saddened by his death: 'There will be mourning, there will be a sense of loss, there will be a sense of us having to bond together to share this tragedy and to support and celebrate his life.'

Daniel Day-Lewis – who was shortly to collect an Oscar for his performance in *There Will Be Blood* – paid his own emotional tribute when he appeared on *The Oprah Winfrey Show*. His eyes filled with tears when he said: 'I hope you don't mind if I speak about this, Oprah... I feel very unsettled at the moment. I only just heard the news about Heath Ledger. It seems strange to be talking about anything else. There isn't anything to say other than to express one's regret to his family and his friends. I didn't know him; I have a strong impression I would have liked him very much as a person if I had. I had already marvelled at some of his work – and looked forward to the work he would do in the future.'

Heath's friend Ellen DeGeneres, who once interviewed him when *Brokeback Mountain* was released and coaxed him into describing in detail his 'clenched' portrayal of Ennis, was equally devastated. At the end of taping her syndicated talk show, soon after his death, she called him, 'an amazing, amazing, talented young man... He was a friend – and we will miss him.' She then ran a hilarious clip of his appearance on the show in which, after talking in depth about his portrayal of Ennis, he joked around with her as they pretended to toboggan downhill at speed.

The Four Feathers' director Shekhar Kapur, whose telephone call Heath never received that fateful Tuesday, paid tribute to his friend and spoke of his health problems, especially his difficulty in sleeping: 'What happens is the doctors give him prescription drugs and in the end he still can't sleep. When you're really stressed out and your body is tired, you wake up after three hours, so you take two more pills – we've all done it at times.' He also said that a great many observers had not judged Heath's career correctly: 'Everyone was saying that here was a star who hadn't handled his career well. They said *Brokeback Mountain* was great, but why didn't he do something more commercial? They didn't really know what he was all about. They said it was interesting that he was going to play the Joker because maybe that was going to make him an international star, not realising that he didn't care about being an international star.'

Many of Heath's admirers had contacted Kapur: 'They've seen maybe one or two of his films but they say they have been crying ever since he died. It's something like what happened with James Dean. After Heath's death, everybody realised that a really important soul had gone. Every time he was offered a part, he would talk to me, and I often saw him rejecting major, major parts. Big directors were pursuing him and whenever I asked him why he had turned one of them down, he said it was because he couldn't be that character. He'd say, "I don't see any moral aspect of that character that, as a human being, I can identify with."' Kapur also recalled the tough desert shoot of *The Four Feathers*: 'Every day I'd say, "I can't handle it, I'm resigning tomorrow." And Heath would always come to me the next morning with a big smile and say, "Where's your resignation letter?" Then he'd slap me on the back and say, "C'mon, let's go," and we'd get in the car and head for the set. He used to call me his elder brother.'

Politicians too were moved by Heath's death. Australian Prime Minister Kevin Rudd commented, 'It is tragic that we have lost one of our nation's finest actors in the prime of his life. Heath Ledger's diverse and challenging roles will be remembered as some of the great performances by an Australian actor.' He also said that the nation's thoughts were with his family and close friends, especially his daughter Matilda.

The most emotive of tributes were those paid by the family – using their intimate nicknames for him – when they placed the notice of his death in their local newspaper, *The West Australian*: 'How do we describe our sudden and tragic loss. You were the most amazing "old soul" in a young man's body. As a close-knit and very private family we have observed you so determined yet quietly travelling in your self-styled path in life, nothing would get in your way... no mountain too tall, no river too wide. You dreamed your dreams and lived them with passion and intelligent commitment. We have been privileged to accompany you on a ride through life that has simply been amazing and through it all we have loved each other beyond imagination.'

The family said his true legacy would be his daughter with actor Michelle Williams, from whom he split the previous year. 'Our hearts are broken...' they added. In a separate notice, father Kim wrote: 'Heatho, Beef ... my beautiful boy, so loving, so talented, so independent ... so no more chess games, mate ... this is it, couldn't beat you anyway. We were one, in soul and commitment, just ... father and son.'

Sister Kate said she could 'hardly breathe' as she tried to write her tribute: 'We were the ultimate soul mates. You were so many things to so many people, but to me you were just my little brother. You will never leave my thoughts, "Roast", ever.'

Younger sister Olivia wrote: 'Heath inspired so many young actors around the world to pursue their dreams. You're my idol, my hero, but most importantly, my loving big brother. I'll treasure every moment we spent together.'

The immediate family said: 'Your true legacy lives on in beautiful little Matilda who will always remain in the greatest of care. Our hearts are broken.'

Even as the people of Perth read the notices, the family was in the process of flying to the US to carry out the task of finalising the American end of the funeral arrangements. The Australian consulate in New York offered them assistance as the body was transferred from the Medical Examiner's office to the Frank E. Campbell funeral chapel – who in their long history had handled the funerals of celebrities such as John Lennon, Judy Garland and James Cagney; there had even been riots outside its old premises when they dealt with the funeral of silent screen star Rudolph Valentino and New York saw scenes of mass hysteria over his death. George Amado, general manager of the funeral home, confirmed arrangements had been completed, but refused to divulge the details: 'The family doesn't want us to give out any information.' Reporters and photographers gathered outside the building and there was also a police presence to prevent any disturbance near the home.

A makeshift memorial outside Heath's SoHo apartment had grown to more than 100 bouquets, along with candles, signs and notes and a computer printout of an Australian flag bore the message: 'We will always be proud of you, Heath. Rest in peace mate. You will be missed.' It was a similar scene in Brooklyn, where many remembered happier times and Heath skateboarding around the area wearing one of his large, woolly hats. Flowers were also left outside his homes in Los Angeles and Perth. His parents and sister Kate arrived in New York at the start of the weekend after an exhausting journey from Western Australia and they, together with Michelle and Matilda, attended a private memorial service in Manhattan.

At 4p.m. on Friday, 25 January 2008, Heath Ledger's body, dressed in a black suit inside his coffin, was placed inside a pine crate and loaded into a black hearse by 5 members of the funeral company staff. Police had to keep a crowd of about 50 paparazzi, eager to get a shot, under control as the manoeuvre was carried out.

On the Saturday night 1,000 guests inside New York's Waldorf Astoria hotel grand ballroom for the *G'Day USA* Australia Day Ball heard a moving letter from Kim Ledger, who had asked Australia's Consul-General in New York, John Olsen, to read it out loud to guests. 'Heath is, and always will be, an Australian,' he wrote. 'He adored his home. His last two weeks with us over Christmas in Perth were just bliss. Heath did not become an actor for the fame or fortune. He loved his craft and he loved helping his friends. He loved chess and skateboarding too. My image of Heath in New York is him with his skateboard, a canvas bag and his beanie. That was Heath to me.'

The ball was designed as a glamour event to celebrate the end of the two-week *G'Day USA* festival in America, promoting everything Australian in the States. Organisers altered the programme to honour Heath and there were tears when a minute's silence was held in his honour. An iconic *Brokeback Mountain* shot of the smiling actor, complete with cowboy hat, was projected onto a screen during the tribute. 'The response we have received here in New York about Heath's tragic passing is certainly an indication that Heath is held in high esteem as an exceptionally talented actor,' Olsen said.

His body was flown to Los Angeles, where it was then taken to Pierce Brothers Westwood Village Memorial Park and Mortuary en route to Perth. The family would still not reveal details of arrangements, but Naomi Watts – who had cancelled an appearance at the première of her film *Funny Games* because of her grief over the loss of her ex-lover – was reported to have joined the Ledgers and Michelle, plus 10 other friends and family including his *Candy* co-star Abbie Cornish, at the funeral home for a service 'after hours' that Saturday evening. When the 30-minute service concluded, the group moved on to the Beverly Hills Hotel for a dinner in a private room. It was a sad occasion but people still managed to smile and hug each other.

By the Wednesday Kim was back in New York to collect his son's possessions from the apartment where his body had been discovered just over a week earlier. He arrived at 10am and was escorted in through a back entrance by security guards before spending an hour inside. Building superintendent Tamba Mossa took him to a small memorial in the garden and basement and when he saw the memorial, made by other residents of the block, he stopped and said: 'It's beautiful.' He then had to fly to the West Coast once more for a moving private ceremony where Heath's Hollywood friends could mourn his passing.

The event took place on the Sony lot in Culver City and a galaxy of stars, mostly in black, joined the family for the 90-minute service. Hundreds of mourners, many with tears in their eyes, saw images of Heath on a giant screen and listened to Todd Haynes, director of the *Dylan* film, pay tribute to his friend and colleague. 'It was a very loving tribute – emotional and loving,' one of the mourners said. 'At times it was very sad and then there were some lighter moments. The service was a very simple, moving tribute from family and people who had worked with him.'

It was a measure of the esteem and affection in which the young actor was held that the ceremony attracted so many notable figures from the film world. Kim Ledger told the assembled throng, including Tom Cruise and his wife Katie Holmes plus scores of other household names, that Michelle apologised for not being at the service with Matilda and Ben Harper, accompanied by a string quartet, performed a song he had written especially to commemorate his close friend. Ellen DeGeneres and her partner Portia de Rossi attended, as did Naomi Watts, who wore a simple black outfit, dark glasses and a silver cross around her neck. Among the other mourners were Oscar winner Sean Penn, Josh Hartnett and Heath's *Lords of Dogtown* co-star, Emile Hirsch. Shannyn Sossamon, co-star in two of his films, Gemma Ward, Lily Cole and Lindsay Lohan were also there, as well as Orlando Bloom and Sienna Miller, who had both starred with him in different films.

Throughout the day there was, of course, a high level of security and police manned the main gate to the studio while an army of security guards wearing dark suits and hi-tech ear-pieces continually patrolled the perimeter of the building where the ceremony was held.

From there, the exhausted and emotionally drained

Ledger family and friends flew overnight from the Tom Bradley Terminal of Los Angeles International Airport to Brisbane and landed on the morning of Tuesday, 5 February, en route to Perth to begin the final arrangements for the funeral in Heath's hometown, where they were joined the next day by Michelle Williams and Matilda.

Even as the family assembled, the apartment where Heath died was back on the rental market at £12,500 a month. One agent pragmatically said, 'It will rent quickly. What happened there will have no effect on that.'

There was massive media interest in that weekend's events – a memorial service followed by a private funeral on the Saturday – and Kim Ledger appealed to the press pack outside the family home: 'It's a pretty sad time and we are finding it difficult to cope by ourselves. The funeral will be very, very private and there will only be 10 people there, immediate family and nobody else.'

What the family were planning, however, was to hold a wake on the Saturday at a Colonial-style waterfront restaurant, the Indiana Tea House at Cottesloe Beach: the resort village south of Perth and an area much-loved by Heath. As preparations continued, the news came from America to confirm what the family maintained all along: Heath's death was an accident. But the events that were to take place on Saturday, 9 February were to be as remarkable as the life of the man remembered and celebrated that day.

Floral tributes, including Australian native flowers and bouquets of lilies, began arriving before 9p.m. and the card on one bouquet read: 'In honour of the love and light Heath brought to the world, he will never be forgotten.' A haunting Aboriginal dirge played on a didgeridoo (a traditional wind instrument) by local musician Levi Islam greeted the mourners when they arrived at the chapel of Penrhos College girls' school (the name means 'peak of the moor' in Welsh), a few kilometres from the home of Heath's mother, Sally.

Michelle Williams, in a white dress with black trim and wearing dark glasses, arrived with a police escort in a six-car cavalcade with Heath's parents and sister. Supporting each other, Michelle and Kate entered the chapel for the 75-minute service. Heath's mother Sally had to be helped by her husband Roger. Mourners, including Gemma Ward and Naomi Watts, had to pass through security checks before entering the chapel and the small windows of the building were blocked to prevent pictures being taken from outside or the media peering in. Throughout the service family photographs of Heath were shown and there was also a slide-show tribute to Matilda, who was not at the funeral.

She played a part in her own way, though, as 'Happy Ever After', written for her by Ben Harper, was played as the montage was shown. The images of Matilda – who bears a striking likeness to her father – were a heartbreaking reminder to those present of Heath's absence. Cate Blanchett gave a moving and, at times, amusing eulogy to him and Kim, Sally and Kate all spoke, as did *Candy* director Neil Armfield. Among the Australian actors at the service were Bryan Brown, Michael Caton, Joel Edgerton, Rose Byrne and Shane Jacobson.

The programme read: 'This room is filled with the love we all felt for a great friend who will be missed by all of us. We want to thank those of you who took care of him and participated in his beautiful life.'

His favourite music was played, including 'The Times They Are A-Changin'' by Bob Dylan, Powderfinger's 'These Days' and Pink Floyd's 'Wish You Were Here'. The service ended with the sound of John Lennon's voice on the classic 'Come Together' track by The Beatles. A group of 10 then went to the Fremantle Cemetery to scatter his ashes in a family plot where two of his grandparents lay.

As day turned into night, the mourners assembled at the Indiana Tea House to talk of their memories of Heath and their sadness at his loss. But then something remarkable happened: a group, some family and some friends, wandered down to the water's edge of the beach where Heath had spent so many happy hours. One by one they entered the surf, arm in arm, some still in the mourning clothes they had worn hours earlier at the chapel, others stripping down to their underwear. Rose Byrne was among a group who got soaked but didn't care and Michelle, hiding her sad eyes behind sunglasses, was dragged into the water too, laughing as the waves pounded around her.

Heath's father Kim looked down from the restaurant balcony at the young crowd, laughing and enjoying life in the same way that his beloved son had enjoyed life to the full. The sun sank slowly in the distance, casting a beautiful pink glow as the sound of laughter travelled across the sands that he had known and loved for so long; it was a fitting end to a brief, but astonishingly full life – a finale that Heath Ledger would no doubt have approved of.

EPILOGUE

The real tragedy of Heath Ledger's death was, of course, that a young man of just twenty eight summers should die long before his time. His family will continue to mourn and, heartbreakingly, a tiny girl, his beloved daughter Matilda, will grow up not knowing her father.

The fact that he was a film star and that the movie world and the audiences who flock to the cinema would also suffer loss, is, in a way, insignificant in comparison. Yet it was that fame that made Heath Ledger the iconic figure he was in life and will continue to be in death.

His performance in *Brokeback Mountain* earned comparisons with a young Marlon Brando. His death at such a tender age inevitably left people saying that he should also be likened to James Dean, the star of *Rebel Without a Cause* who died behind the wheel of his car aged just 25 over half a century before Heath passed away. In death Heath Ledger joined that 'club' of Dean, Marilyn Monroe and Buddy Holly; stars who would never grow old.

In a mere decade his body of work ranged from action films with historic settings to a microscopic examination of drug-addicted lovers, from Pythonesque humour to the achingly poignant beauty of *Brokeback*.

What would have happened to him in the years ahead will never be known. Heath Ledger wrote poetry, was involved in music at every level and was keen to move behind the camera and direct. He no doubt would have succeeded in everything he tried. He was that sort of man.

FILMOGRAPHY

The Dark Knight (2008)
I'm Not There (2007)
Candy (2006)
Casanova (2005)
Brokeback Mountain
   (2005)
The Brothers Grimm
   (2005)
Lords Of Dogtown (2005)
The Sin Eater (2003)
Ned Kelly (2003)
The Four Feathers (2002)
Monster's Ball (2001)
A Knight's Tale (2001)
The Patriot (2000)
Two Hands (1999)

10 Things I Hate About
   You (1999)
Roar (TV series) (1997)
Home And Away (TV
   series) (1997)
Paws (1997)
Blackrock (1997)
Sweat (TV series) (1996)
Ship To Shore (TV series)
   (1993)
Clowning Around (1992)